Macmillan USA, Inc.
201 West 103rd Street
Indianapolis, IN 46290

A Pearson Education Company

Jeff Davidson

10 Minute Guide to Stress Management

Copyright © 2001 by Macmillan USA, Inc.

International Standard Book Number: 0-02-863995-2
Library of Congress Catalog Card Number: Available upon request.

03 02 01   8 7 6 5 4 3 2 1

Interpretation of the printing code: The rightmost number of the first series of numbers is the year of the book's printing; the rightmost number of the second series of numbers is the number of the book's printing. For example, a printing code of 01-1 shows that the first printing occurred in 2001.

Printed in the United States of America

Note: This publication contains the opinions and ideas of its author. It is intended to provide helpful and informative material on the subject matter covered. It is sold with the understanding that the author and publisher are not engaged in rendering professional services in the book. If the reader requires personal assistance or advice, a competent professional should be consulted.

CONTENTS

Introduction

Welcome to the *10 Minute Guide to Stress Management*. Although you've read other stress management books and articles, this one is different:

- It's slim, very slim, because you don't have a lot of time to wade through voluminous text.

- It offers the essence of what you need to effectively manage stress.

- Instead of chapters, there are lessons—each designed to give you key background information and action-oriented tips.

- Each lesson only takes about 10 minutes to complete.

In this book, you learn about the nature of stress, why it's so subjective, what happens to your body when you're stressed, how to stay in control more often, and how to minimize the effects of stress in general. You also learn about the critical need for sleep and staying balanced, how to avoid the overspend/overwork syndrome, and how to limit the effects of procrastination. The overarching goal is to keep stress at acceptable levels, to be more effective in handling pressure-packed situations, and in general, to keep your career and life in balance.

You will not have to endure ...

- Long lists of steps you have to take.

- Complicated maneuvers.

- Steadfast rules that really don't address the challenges you encounter.

Instead, without much effort, you learn simple but effective techniques for staying in control in situations that might otherwise throw you out of kilter. The techniques presented can all be adapted to better prepare you for the situation you face.

As with all of the books in the *10 Minute Guide* series, every lesson is geared to take only a short time so that you can complete each lesson in about 10 minutes. The whole program takes less than three hours and can easily be completed in a matter of days. So let's get started!

ACKNOWLEDGMENTS

Thanks to Marie Butler-Knight for her continuing brilliance and expertise in overseeing the ever-expanding Macmillan line of excellent lifestyle books. Thanks to my editors, Renee Wilmeth, Tom Stevens, and JoAnna Kremer.

Thanks to Lucy Melvin, Matt Mullen, Christie Koch, and Jennifer Feinman for original writing, proofing, and all-around editorial excellence in helping to get the manuscript to the publisher on time with very little stress. Thanks to Sharon Askew for expert proofreading. Finally, thanks to Valerie Davidson, age 10, for helping daddy to understand the importance of playing every night, and to Kitty and Bunny for being good companions to Valerie.

TRADEMARKS

All terms mentioned in this book that are known to be or are suspected of being trademarks or service marks have been appropriately capitalized. Macmillan USA, Inc., cannot attest to the accuracy of this information. Use of a term in this book should not be regarded as affecting the validity of any trademark or service mark.

LESSON 1
What Is Stress?

In this lesson, you learn about stress, its many causes, and how our bodies react to the circumstances of stress.

WHAT YOUR STRESS CAN TEACH YOU

Please take out a number-two pencil. I'm going to start with a quiz:

> A century ago, when people ate something that didn't agree with them, other than mix a bicarbonate of soda, what else did they do?

No looking on anyone else's paper—you're only cheating yourself.

> Answer: They did not eat that item again.

Today, by comparison, if you eat a pepperoni pizza and you get heartburn, but you still like pepperoni pizza, chances are you'll keep eating pepperoni pizza in the future. Why? As long as you can take some over-the-counter remedy that patches you up, you have little chance of learning not to eat it.

So it is with stress. If popping some pills gets you through the rough parts of the day, then you never learn to master what stresses you. This book is about learning to master stress, and this first lesson involves learning about the nature of stress so that you are in a better position to master the beast.

ALL STRESSED UP AND NO PLACE TO GO

Brian is a sales manager with a large corporation. A few weeks ago, a reorganization was announced. His job now requires that he oversee the work of twice the number of team members he was responsible for before. Suddenly his voice mail seems to always be full. No matter how much he tries to keep up, there are always e-mails that require his attention. To top it off, his boss called him into the office the other day and chastised him for his team's failure to meet last month's sales quota.

Brian stays late at work every day but worries that he is still not completing the necessary tasks. The sun usually sets by the time he makes the long commute home and walks in the door, feet dragging, late for dinner. Beyond his worries about increased pressures at work, Brian is troubled that he doesn't have enough time to spend with his family. Brian's son is not doing well in school, and his wife wants to go on a family vacation.

Soon Brian begins to dread the day ahead of him as the alarm clock wakes him each morning. Sleeping becomes difficult. He chews antacids by the roll in an effort to combat severe heartburn. Because of his upset stomach, he feels little desire to eat. His wife tells him that he has become very irritable and snappish lately.

STRESS IN A HIGH-SPEED WORLD

Brian's experience is common in today's high-speed world. With the pressures of the modern job, the demands of family life, and nearly constant change, it is no wonder many people suffer from the symptoms of stress.

Stress impacts on healthcare in the following ways:

- 75 percent to 90 percent of visits to physicians are stress-related.

- Job stress is a major health factor, costing businesses an estimated $150 billion annually.

- Stress-related disorders are a major cause of rapidly increasing healthcare costs.

Source: National Mental Health Institute

Moreover, a recent report by the National Institute for Occupational Safety and Health indicates that more doctors and researchers are discovering connections between high levels of stress and long-term health problems, such as cardiovascular disease and workplace injuries (see Lesson 4, "Managing Office Stress").

CHRONIC STRESS

Chronic stress is a specific, serious type of stress disorder and may require professional help. Chronic stress is an unrelenting and constant part of the sufferer's life. Often a person is so used to this type of stress that he or she does not even recognize the symptoms because of their constant presence over the years. Chronic stress can arise from feeling trapped in an unhappy marriage or a hated career, for example.

PLAIN ENGLISH

Chronic stress   Long-term, unrelenting, potentially health- or life-threatening stress that often becomes unrecognized by the victim.

Chronic stress may also stem from childhood trauma or a troubling way of looking at the world. Someone who has a problem with chronic stress often does not see a way out of suffering. Chronic stress, in serious cases, may even lead to suicide, violence, or death through stroke or heart attack. Persons who think they might have this more serious type of stress disorder should seek help from a professional counselor.

CAUTION

If you believe that you suffer from chronic stress, put down this book and call a medical advisor.

A CHAIN REACTION

To control the negative effects of stress in your life, it is first necessary to understand how stress affects your body, and how you can manage stress in different areas of your life. Why does stress affect so many people? What are some of its causes? And what initiates a stress reaction?

When your brain perceives danger, it sets a biological chain reaction in motion, releasing chemicals into your body that put your nervous system in high gear. In other words, your heart pumps faster and your breathing accelerates to take in extra oxygen. Your muscles tense up and your senses feel sharpened. Believe it or not, your blood actually clots faster!

These physiologic reactions are important because they enable the human body to deal with a threatening situation. Your reflexes are ready to help you escape the perceived danger, or to fight if necessary—this is often called the *fight-or-flight response.*

PLAIN ENGLISH

> **Physiologic**   Consistent with an organism's normal or expected functioning.
>
> **Fight-or-flight response**   An automatic response to stimuli, real or perceived, that enables the human body to deal with a threatening situation.

This biological response was an asset to ancient man. If he were walking through the jungle and sensed danger, let's say a hungry tiger standing in the middle of the path ahead, his body would instantly respond to help him avoid being tiger chow.

NO TIGERS FOR BATTLE

Ancient man would be prepared to fight the tiger (which would be messy unless it were a small tiger) or run away to safety (which also would be messy unless it were a slow tiger). Ultimately, the stress response evolved to help humans survive in dangerous situations.

Presumably, there are no tigers prowling about the cubicles in your workplace, or if you work at home, there are none lounging under your kitchen table. However, stress can be useful for modern man as well. It can motivate us to accomplish tasks within a tight deadline. It may help us to work quickly with increased focus.

THE STRESS RESPONSE AT WORK

Suppose your department introduces a new type of software, and you have to learn it in a matter of days. You're comfortable with the old program, and you don't want to take on the new, but you have no choice but to learn it unless you want to be left behind.

So what do you do? You put all of your energy and intensity into the effort. At the same time, your stress level helps you rise to the task. The stress you feel helps you master the new software quickly.

For the next three days, however (at work, at lunch, at home, and all points in between), many of your internal systems are revving at high levels to accomplish the task at hand. You begin to get that feeling that some people describe as "stressed out" or "burned out." Stress, then, can be good in some cases but bad in other cases.

CAUTION
A problem can arise if you are "on" all the time.

Long-term stress contributes to serious long-term health conditions, such as heart problems, high blood pressure, ulcers, and mental effects.

Stress prevents the body from resting, which can decrease productivity at work. While you are sleeping, your mind is not. You can think that you are getting enough sleep because you were in bed for eight hours, but if you are stressed out, you are actually not able to reach the deeper levels of sleep necessary to keep you from feeling groggy (see Lesson 6, "Getting Sleep, Staying in Balance").

Stress also affects concentration and adds to laziness and clumsiness. Stress prevents you from focusing on anything other than what is causing the stress. As a result, people under stress often ignore hobbies and other things that are necessary for personal pleasure and for the very relaxation that might decrease stress levels. .

WHEN STRESS KNOCKS ON YOUR DOOR

What separates "good" stress from "bad" stress, and how can you tell them apart or know when stress is becoming a problem for you?

Short, intense periods of stress sometimes can be motivating or thrilling and, if managed properly, are not threats to your long-term well-being. This type of stress is called *acute stress.* It usually is recognized by the individual, and the symptoms of this kind of stress are apparent. Some of the symptoms, as adapted from the book *The Stress Solution,* by Lyle Miller and Alma Dell Smith, include ...

- Anger or irritability.

- Anxiety.

- Depression.

- Muscular problems, or pains or tensions that lead to pulled muscles.

- Headaches.

- Elevated blood pressure, rapid heartbeat, sweaty palms, and heart palpitations.

- Dizziness and migraine headaches.

- Cold hands or feet.

- Shortness of breath.

- Chest pains.

TIP

Stress can also show up as stomach and bowel problems, such as heartburn, sour stomach, diarrhea, constipation, or—perhaps worst of all—excessive flatulence!

If you spend your days worrying and suffering from headaches and constipation, you certainly won't enjoy life to the fullest.

CAUTION

To make matters worse, experiencing stress symptoms often leads to more worrying or troubling thoughts that can in turn increase the tension in your life.

Suppose you are worried about that new software program at work you have to master in three days. You begin to experience a constant headache, which slows you down. You then have to stay later at work, which upsets your spouse. Your headache makes you irritable, and you snap at your spouse. Your spat with your spouse further distracts you from the task at hand the next day, which slows you down, creates tension, adds to your headache, and makes you stay late at work. Your stress level can increase and further add to the downward cycle in which you are caught.

WHEN STRESS IS GOOD FOR YOU

When you think of stress, you may recall pressure from a project at work, being forced to stay late and having to meet the expectations of a demanding boss. Or you might remember a time when you were in college and had to stay up all night studying for that crucial final exam. In such instances, stress can sometimes be good, in moderation, allowing you to perform in deadline situations and maintain focus—or, for some people, providing a thrill or excitement. This other type of stress on the body is known as *eustress*.

PLAIN ENGLISH

Eustress   Beneficial stress that enables people to function more effectively, maintain concentration, strive to meet challenges, or seek thrills or excitement.

TIP

Some people can be energized by stress—not just at the workplace, but also in certain recreational pursuits that thrill the daredevil in them. Bungee jumping from a bridge is one extreme example.

Paula Gomes, Psy.D., Licensed Clinical Psychologist and former director of the Faculty and Staff Assistance Program at the Johns Hopkins Medical Institutions says, "Positive stress may be experienced when buying a house, having a baby, getting married, etc. Although these are stressful life events, they impact us positively—not in the same way as unhealthy stress does." A positive event, such as a wedding, can be stressful in a positive way, although the bride and groom may not agree that it is at the time.

TIP

Stress is a relative term. It can mean different things, depending on the situation, or even depending on the person.

Different people may have different levels of tolerance for stress. Or what may be stressful to one person is not necessarily stressful to another. Let's look at Greg and his wife, Diedre. Greg is an organized person. He likes to have plans for the weekend getaway to the beach laid out completely and thoroughly before he leaves. He makes hotel reservations weeks in advance and calls to double-check them before leaving—right after he checks the oil, transmission fluid, and battery level in the car for the third time.

TIP

Different stimuli trigger stress in different people.

Diedre is more of a free spirit. (Hey, opposites attract!) She would prefer that they didn't have a hotel reservation—while looking for a place to stay, they could have a new adventure or discover a new place. What might cause extreme stress in Greg, such as losing the written itinerary for the trip, wouldn't bother Diedre in the least.

WHEN DOES STRESS BECOME TOO MUCH?

How can you identify when stress is unhealthy for you? Aside from experiencing any of the symptoms discussed in this lesson, ask yourself the following questions, compiled by the National Mental Health Association:

- Do minor problems and disappointments upset me excessively?
- Do the small pleasures of life fail to satisfy me?
- Am I unable to stop thinking of my worries?
- Do I feel inadequate and suffer from self-doubt?
- Am I constantly tired?
- Do I experience flashes of anger over situations that used to not bother me?
- Have I noticed a change in my sleeping or eating patterns?
- Do I suffer from chronic pain, headaches, or backaches?

CAUTION

Don't ignore the symptoms of stress if they begin to have a constant negative impact on your life. If they go unchecked, they can lead to serious medical conditions, such as high blood pressure and heart attacks.

Dr. Gomes says,

> *Stress is unhealthy when it begins to take a toll on one's physical and emotional well-being and starts affecting different aspects of one's life. If individuals find themselves emotionally on edge all the time, depressed, anxious, or having problems at work or in their normal relationships, or having physical symptoms, such as sleep disturbance or appetite changes, they must begin to examine the unhealthy aspects of their lives.*

You might find yourself working on an ongoing project for work, and the stress it causes follows you home and causes problems between you and your spouse or children. Or if you have trouble getting along with co-workers, this probably indicates that you need to find a way to deal with your stress.

In the following lessons, you learn more about the many causes of stress, how stress affects the human body, and different methods for managing stress. Simple techniques range from prioritizing and scheduling to time-honored practices such as meditation and yoga, which can give you an increased sense of balance and control.

THE 30-SECOND RECAP

- If you suspect that you suffer from chronic stress, which is an unrelenting and constant part of your life, seek help right away.

- Some level of stress affects most individuals in their daily lives.

- Recognizing the sources of stress and its overall effect on your life allows you to better work toward stress management.

- Short, intense periods of stress sometimes can be motivating or thrilling and, if managed properly, are not threats to your long-term well-being.

- You can manage stress and its effects on your life by working with some simple techniques.

Lesson 2

How Does Stress Show Up?

In this lesson, you learn more ways that stress can show up in your life, and how it can have long-term effects on your health and well-being.

Science Finally Offers Recognition

In the 1930s, an endocrinologist named Dr. Hans Selye conducted studies showing that organisms exhibit a biological response to sensory experiences called *stressors.* Dr. Selye observed that experiences classified as stressors are generally unpleasant situations the body responds to with a series of reactions that prepare it for fight or flight (see Lesson 1, "What Is Stress?"). Even after Western medicine recognized stress, it was many decades before the medical establishment began to grasp the far-reaching ramifications of it.

PLAIN ENGLISH

Stressor   An undesirable or unpleasant situation the body responds to with fight-or-flight reactions.

In the late 1970s, Dr. Herbert Benson demonstrated that meditation could induce direct physical benefits, such as reduced muscle tension, decreased heart rate, and lower blood pressure (more on meditation in Lesson 13, "Meditation"). In his book *The Relaxation Response,* Dr. Benson discusses his belief that the "core of meditation" is what he calls the *relaxation response,* which represents the body's innate physiological mechanism that actually diminishes or prevents one's fight or flight process—that is, one's stress response.

THE STRESS-IMMUNITY LINK

In 1991, the psychologist Sheldon Cohen did a study that showed that people who said they experience high stress levels may suffer from weakened immune systems as a result. When repeated in 1998, the study reported the same results. Researchers found that subjects experiencing long-term, chronic stress were three to five times more likely to get sick.

CAUTION

Subjects in Dr. Cohen's study who scored high on a scale of *perceived* stress also were more likely to catch a cold when infected by researchers with a virus than those who did not score high. Hence, perceived stress is potentially as disruptive as tangible, identifiable stress.

Another researcher, immunologist Ronald Glaser, studied individuals caring for spouses with dementia. Glaser found that the caregivers experienced diminished antibody production when exposed to an influenza vaccine. Presumably, the caregivers experienced ongoing stress as a result of the day-to-day responsibilities and worries associated with caring for a chronically ill family member. This stress resulted in the breakdown of the body's immune system.

THE FLOODGATES OPEN

Health experts now realize that stress can have major effects on a person's well-being. According to Dr. Pamela Peeke of the University of Maryland, "The human body was never meant to deal with prolonged chronic stress. We weren't meant to drag around bad memories, anxieties, and frustrations."

Doctors and researchers continue to study the negative effects of stress and have shown how the body reacts to perceived dangers. Other studies have found an association between chronic stress and heart disease. A study involving monkeys found those experiencing more stress also had higher rates of heart disease. In other cases, researchers also linked stress to obesity and high blood pressure.

TIP

> Recognizing stress in your life may enable you to control other health risks.

THE BODY'S IMMEDIATE RESPONSE TO STRESS

You know how your body feels when you anticipate danger or you are nervous. You get a rush of adrenaline when slamming on the brakes to avoid the careless driver who cut you off. You feel the butterflies in your stomach before giving that important presentation to the executives of your company. What processes are going on in your body when you experience these sensations?

Presumably, when prehistoric man encountered a hungry tiger, alarm bells went off in his body. Whether you see a free-roaming hungry tiger or your boss coming to ask you to stay late on a Friday, the reaction is the same (although perhaps on a different level).

How does your body prepare you for an alarming situation that requires focus and immediate action?

Let's say it's Friday and time to leave work. You're packing your briefcase and clearing your desk, thinking of dinner. Then you peer above the cubicle walls and see your boss on the opposite side of the room. He's making his way slowly through the maze of cubicles, and you know he is coming to ask you to stay late and work on a project of immensely meaningless proportions.

You must escape! But how? Your body goes through the following processes to help you take action:

- When you see your boss coming, your medulla oblongata secretes adrenaline, which floods your body.

- The cortex of your adrenal gland secretes cortisol. (Cortisol regulates metabolism and immunity, and can be toxic over time.) Released cortisol makes you impervious to pain. Your thinking actually improves!

- The pupils of your eyes dilate, enabling you to better see your boss's approach.

- The hair on your body stands on end. (This may be the result of an evolutionary adaptation that makes animals appear bigger to their enemies.)

- Your digestion system shuts down to divert all energy to your muscles.

- Your spleen allows extra red blood cells to flow, carrying more oxygen to your muscles.

- Your liver converts glycogen (stored energy in the form of fat) to glucose (fuel) to give you more energy.

- Your lungs take in more oxygen.

- Your heart rate and blood pressure rise.

You are now fully aware, energized, and ready to go. Meanwhile, as a result of your immediate response to the stressor, your immune system's infection-fighting ability is significantly reduced.

THE BODY'S DELAYED RESPONSE TO STRESS

Suppose you have mega-plans for this evening and will not be detained for even one minute! You crouch down and follow a path, away from your boss, through the cubicle maze. You get to the exit, undetected, and make your way out of the building. You walk briskly, looking over your shoulder to ensure that no one in particular is watching you. Your departure is clean!

Soon your body begins to recover from the fight-or-flight response that occurred when you saw your boss approaching. Your breathing slows and your heart rate decreases. In your brain, the hippocampus, a center of memory and learning, is activated to process your body's recovery. Other delayed reactions take effect, each helping to stabilize you from all of the excitement.

What if you see your boss coming to ask you to stay late nearly every night? Or what if you have other frequent stressors in your life? If the fight-or-flight response occurs frequently, it begins to have negative effects on your body. Your brain may be affected by the toxic cortisol secreted by your cortex, and you may experience impaired memory and cognitive ability as a result. Your immune system may become weakened.

The constant lack of blood flow—as a result of the digestive system shutdown during your heightened state—may strain under-nourished cells in your intestines. Constant elevated blood pressure and heart rate may damage blood vessels and mucus lining and cause ulcers.

CAUTION

> Although the stress response can help you when you must take quick action, frequent activation of your body's reactions to stress can begin to deteriorate your health.

A TOLL ON THE BODY AND MIND

Repeatedly high stress levels can cause you to feel run-down and old. Stress can cause aches and pains, and affect your peace of mind. Often, a stressed-out person loses interest in outside activities or hobbies.

CAUTION

> Prolonged stress can even prompt thoughts of suicide.

Myriad short-term and long-term health and mental problems can result from excessive stress, including increased blood pressure, nausea, insomnia, fatigue, pain, depression, jumpiness, forgetfulness, anger, reduced creativity, and reduced productivity.

TIP

> Get slender. Extra body fat may induce stress. The body draws on fat reserves near the liver for energy during the stress reaction. Researchers have hypothesized that the body stores this fatty fuel near the liver or the middle of the body so that it can be metabolized quickly.

STRESS, GENDER, AND CHILDHOOD EXPERIENCES

Certain people may be more disposed to be affected by stress. You probably know at least one person who always seems to "have it together," or is calm, cool, and collected in the face of turmoil. And you probably know at least one person who's a real hothead. Every little perceived threat or frustration has him either biting back words of rage or running around in a frenzy like the proverbial chicken with a misplaced head.

Studies confirm that, indeed, some people are only moderately affected by stress, while others hit the roof every time something goes wrong.

VENUSIAN AND MARTIAN STRESS REACTIONS

Also, fundamental differences may exist between men and women. Perhaps as a child you remember going to your mother when you broke that garage window with the baseball. You went to your mother instead of your father, because mom would be less likely to be upset. A study at Ohio State University found that women's blood pressure rises less than men's in response to an objective stressor.

Other research, however, suggests that, as a whole, women may feel more stress than men. Ronald Kessler did a Harvard study and found that women feel stress more often because they generally take a more far-reaching view of life. For example, women may worry about many things at a time, while many men can compartmentalize their worries, dealing with only one problem or stressor before moving on to the next one.

THROUGH THE LOOKING GLASS

Childhood experiences may also have an effect on how a person deals with stress. A child raised in a stressful environment, with violence or verbal abuse, will become more susceptible to stress later in life.

CAUTION

As children of stressful upbringings age, they will be so accustomed to high adrenaline levels that they will feel uncomfortable or bored when their body is in a state of calm!

In contrast, a child raised in a healthy or low-stress environment will be less susceptible to stress later in life. Dr. Frank Treiber of the Medical College of Georgia observes that "... if you come from a family that's somewhat chaotic, unstable, not cohesive, and harboring grudges, very early on, it's associated later with greater blood-pressure reactivity to various types of stress."

TIP

Depending on your personal history or your current household environment, you may be more or less susceptible to stress.

STRESS: IS IT ALL IN YOUR HEAD?

John Welwood, Ph.D., thinks that much of the stress people experience can be attributed to constantly trying to fit an internal image of themselves with the image they show the outside world. For example, if a person has a problem handling anger, she might try to be an overly nice person instead of dealing with her problem.

CAUTION

> Constantly monitoring the external self you present to
> the world may result in added stress and anxiety for you.
> So be yourself.

Welwood believes that we all need to open ourselves up to the way we
really feel inside. From there, you can acknowledge your personality
traits for what they really are. This uniformly relieves anxieties associated with trying to be something or somebody who doesn't represent
the genuine you.

TIP

> Maintaining an open mind as we approach our surround-
> ings can reduce anxiety by enabling us to meet whatever
> arises without holding to any fixed idea about what it
> means or how it should unfold.

Stress is relieved as the person feels no internal pressure to conform to
a false image of how he or she is supposed to appear or act in given
situations as they arise.

THE 30-SECOND RECAP

- Only in recent decades has medical science begun to understand the body's physiologic responses to stress and their
  impact on our health.

- Research shows that the side effects of stress are a threat to
  long-term health.

- A person's susceptibility to stress depends on many factors,
  including gender, personal history, and self-image.

- The better you understand yourself and the less internal pressure you feel to conform to a false image of yourself, the
  more easily and naturally you will be able to avoid the impact
  of potentially stressful situations.

LESSON 3
The Toxic Workplace

In this lesson, you learn why much of the stress you experience in the workplace may be organizationally induced, and you get tips as a manager or staff worker for carving a saner path.

IT'S A JUNGLE IN THERE

New projects, new tasks, a new e-mail about that old project—the tasks add up and threaten to choke you with an ever-deepening sensation of stress. With rising deadline pressure, the frustrations of constantly evolving technology, and the increasing challenges in management, the modern workplace has many employees feeling constantly stressed. Every day feels like a fight to survive in a jungle-like environment.

PLAIN ENGLISH

> **Job stress** The physical and emotional response to harmful working conditions, including circumstances in which the job requirements exceed the capabilities, resources, or needs of the worker.

THE NUMBER-ONE HEALTH RISK

Increasing numbers of career professionals report that job stress is the leading cause of personal stress. Only recently have studies directly assessed the effects of job stress on personal health. According to Princeton Survey Research Associates, "Three-fourths of employees believe the worker has more on-the-job stress than a generation ago." In a study by Northwestern National Life, 40 percent of workers report that their job is "very or extremely stressful."

PLAIN ENGLISH

Cardiovascular	Pertaining to the heart and blood vessels.

The Encyclopedia of Occupational Safety and Health reports that disease, musculoskeletal disorders, and psychological disorders are all linked to job stress. Researchers are still exploring the probable connections between job stress and increased risk for workplace injury, suicide, cancer, ulcers, and impaired immune function.

CAUTION

All of these findings and inquiries attest to the long-term detrimental effects of job stress on the working individual.

THE PRICE WE PAY

According to a study by the National Institute for Occupational Safety and Health (NIOSH), job stress accounts for a high volume of health problems reported in the United States. A statistic taken from the *Journal of Occupational and Environmental Medicine* shows that "Health care expenditures are nearly 50 percent greater for workers who report high levels of stress."

In simpler terms, people who work in stressful jobs cost the healthcare economy *1.5 times that of the average unstressed worker.* And this is without consideration of the other economic costs directly resulting from stressed workers, such as decreased productivity. Essentially, the economic costs of job stress are not limited to healthcare costs; they affect the overall economy.

AN ORGANIZATIONAL CULTURE OF STRESS

If you're a manager or supervisor, this lesson may alter your view of your workplace and how to foster a more nurturing environment. If you have responsibility at work solely for yourself, you nevertheless will gain insights about the degree to which stress in the workplace is endemic to early twenty-first century organizations.

For years, much attention has been given to the concept of job stress as an individual problem. The symptoms of job stress have been limited to recognizable characteristics in individual workers. The results of job stress have been understood primarily on the same level—that of the individual worker.

CAUTION

> Job stress is an American workplace phenomenon, and job stress pervades the entire fabric of many work environments, affecting the performance of entire organizations and the overall economy in general!

NIOSH reports that either the individual manages the working stress conditions and decreases the risk of injury or illness, or the individual succumbs to the pressures of the situation and falls prey to the job stress, thus resulting in risk of injury or illness.

Job stress no longer only affects the individual worker, who may lose a job due to an inability to perform all the required tasks. Job stress also affects the organization as a whole—its performance in the market may be jeopardized by internal problems with job stress.

CULPRITS FOR JOB STRESS

Many job conditions within an organization can lead to job stress. Here are some particular culprits that tend to induce job stress:

- **The design of tasks**   Heavy workload; infrequent rest breaks; long work hours and shiftwork; and hectic and routine tasks that have little inherent meaning, do not use workers' skills, and provide little sense of control.

- **Management style**   Lack of participation by workers in decision-making, poor communication in the organization, and lack of family-friendly policies.

- **Interpersonal relationships** Poor social environment and lack of support or help from co-workers and supervisors.

- **Work roles** Conflicting or uncertain job expectations, too much responsibility, too many "hats to wear."

- **Career concerns** Job insecurity and lack of opportunity for growth, advancement, or promotion; rapid changes for which workers are unprepared.

- **Environmental conditions** Unpleasant or dangerous physical conditions, such as crowding, noise, air pollution, or ergonomics problems.

PRODUCTIVITY PLUS

Understandably, a key goal in any organization is to operate effectively and efficiently and to compete successfully in the market. Because companies with healthy workplace policies consistently perform better than others, most organizations and the managers who can effect change need to reconsider their own policies and work to establish a healthier working environment.

Here are several key characteristics for reduced job stress, a healthier workplace, and more motivated workers:

- Recognition of employees' work performance

- Career development opportunities

- An organizational structure and culture that value the individual worker

- Management actions consistent with organizational values

STRESS IN THE STARTUP COMPANY

The growth in Internet startup companies has spawned a whole new job market for employees with computer skills. It also has developed into one of the most stressful fields—one in which companies face the "make it or break it" strains of establishing themselves almost every day.

Let's look at the situation of one worker.

Casey worked for many years as a computer network administrator with a small corporation. Months ago, headhunters approached him and offered him a new position with a Web startup company, which he accepted.

While his salary has nearly doubled, Casey's new job brings him a load of stress. After years in an established office, working regular 40- to 45-hour weeks, his new work schedule is grueling—often 10- to 12-hour days, five or six days a week.

The office environment is different, too. In his old job, Casey and the other employees frequently interacted. Things are stiff and hectic in his new office. Some co-workers would rather send him an e-mail than walk 30 or 40 paces to his office.

CASEY AT THE BAT

Casey knows he is capable of performing his new job, and he is continually learning more. Nevertheless, every day leaves him feeling overworked and burned out. He doesn't feel motivated by the office environment, and increasingly he feels that his new job is at risk.

The young company is facing a rough period. So far the company has done well; however, a new product release is coming up, and the company is behind schedule. Casey feels pressure from all sides. Not only is he dealing with his own job stress, trying to handle an increased workload and a different atmosphere, but now he is faced with the stressful atmosphere of the entire company. If this new product doesn't get released on time and perform successfully in the market, the company may fold.

ALL TOO COMMON

What Casey is experiencing is an increasingly common situation. While he faces challenges of adjusting to his new job, he also faces the difficulties of workplace-related job stress. His new company is too concerned with survival to address the needs of the employees. This might backfire on the company in the near future, though.

> **CAUTION**
>
> Without adequate stress management and some efforts to modify the workplace stress, all of the workers—from upper-level management down to the very lowest spot on the totem pole—will be headed down the road to burnout.

Casey's situation reflects the intricate nature of the job stress experienced by workers today. There are his own situational factors—being new on the job and unaccustomed to the faster pace of a newly forming company—that influence his ability to handle the job. It is the stressful job conditions, however, that truly threaten his performance. Casey is capable of handling his own situation, but he is handling it in a stressful environment. With these overall job conditions, anyone in his company is bound to experience job stress.

TAMING THE BEAST

Many companies and organizations have made efforts to help their employees deal with job stress. Unfortunately, in their efforts to reduce stress among workers, most organizations fail to inspect their role in developing a stressful working environment. Only a comprehensive approach, including a combination of individual stress management and organizational changes, effectively eliminates job stress.

The first component in this process is stress management. This involves educating individuals on ways to manage their stress. Many organizations offer in-house seminars or design stress management counseling programs. These are very effective on the individual level, but for overall improvement, it is necessary to evaluate the structure of the organization and its effects on working conditions.

TIP

If you work in an inherently stressful environment, investigate all programs your organization offers to assist employees in maintaining balance. In addition to seminars and courses, ask about day care, flex time, mental health days, telecommuting, counseling, and any other support programs.

Different companies and organizations use different methods to evaluate and restructure for job-stress reduction. If you're in management and have the opportunity to effect change, your first step is to identify the problem. Have each worker evaluate the workplace to identify stressful conditions and areas for restructuring or policy change.

TIP

The smaller the group, the easier it is to make the evaluation totally inclusive. Sometimes a group meeting to discuss the situation will even suffice. In a larger organization, it might be necessary to establish a task force.

Using the results of your findings, push for new initiatives to change policies or procedures within the workplace—for example, to allow for more family leave or to require that each job position periodically be reevaluated and a reasonable job description developed.

WHEN YOUR BOSS ENCOURAGES WORKAHOLISM

A closing point: What about when your stress, in large part, can be traced directly back to a boss or bosses who encourage workaholism? Get prepared! With great tact and professionalism, say something along the lines of, "I'm really overcommitted right now, and if I take that on, I can't do it justice."

Here are some other helpful responses:

- "I appreciate your confidence in me. I wouldn't want to take this on, knowing my other tasks and responsibilities right now would prohibit me from doing an excellent job."

- "I'd be happy to handle this assignment for you, but realistically I can't do it without forgoing some other things I'm working on. Of tasks *a* and *b,* which would you like me to do? Which can I put aside?"

- "I can do that for you. Will it be okay if I get back to you in the middle of next week? I currently have _____, _____, and _____ in the queue."

- "The number of tasks and complexity of assignments I'm handling are mounting. Perhaps we could look at a two- or four-week scenario of what's most important to you and when the assignments need to be completed, versus what I can realistically handle over that time period."

Dealing with job stress is today's never-ending story. As organizations vie for position or survival, as technology develops and the world around us brings continuous change, the workplace and career professionals who want to remain in balance must change along with it all, particularly if the work environment itself is inherently stressful.

THE 30-SECOND RECAP

- Each worker in a stressful job costs the healthcare economy 1.5 times that of the average unstressed worker.

- Job stress plagues the modern workplace, resulting not only in health risks for individual workers, but in overall poor performance by companies and organizations.

- In most cases, job stress involves stressful working conditions as well as the individual worker's characteristics and circumstances. Thus, effectively managing job stress requires addressing both personal stress management and overall organizational issues.

LESSON 4
Managing Office Stress

In this lesson, you learn about the impact of deadline pressure, the importance of keeping your stress level in check, and simple ways to maintain balance.

INCREASING DEADLINE PRESSURE IS INEVITABLE

Everything in society has sped up as a result of technology and information. This is especially true for life in the office. As societies and work environments rev at a faster pace, so do the individuals within them. With the constant advent of faster computers and more efficient machines, however, the expectations on workers are higher than ever. Communication has become instantaneous. Less time is spent waiting for a reply, because information can travel as fast as an e-mail or a fax.

CAUTION

While once we might have imagined a future full of machines taking over for humans, the present reality is that with greater interconnectivity and more machines populating our offices, we are expected to do even more.

People are always connected to the office somehow, which has resulted in a lack of escape time. Long gone are the days when you were only reachable when you were physically in the office. Thanks to pagers, cellular phones, voice mail, and fax machines, you can no longer hide from the deadlines at work. They ride home with you.

Communication the Average U.S. Household (3.6 People)
Receives Each Week

Type	Number
Phone calls	54
Mail	35
E-mail	16
Voice mail	4
Cell phone calls	3
Pages	2
Faxes	1

Note: The numbers are even larger for a high-volume household.

Deadline pressure is as inevitable as the advent of a computer that is faster than the last, or a cellular phone that has better reception than the current model. Deadline pressure filters down through the hierarchy at the office.

If extra pressure is being put on your boss, chances are that *his* boss is being pressured. Chances are even greater that *you'll* be pressured. Pressure can also come from within. People constantly raise their expectations of their own performance.

As the speed of office communication and correspondence increases, so does the speed at which deadlines must be met! Everyone is expected to move at a faster pace, while still working with the constant resources of time and money.

CAUTION

People constantly put undue pressure on themselves by worrying about whether they are meeting other people's expectations.

The Importance of Keeping Stress Levels in Check

Increases in deadline pressure often bring about increases in stress levels. The more you have to get done, the more stress your mind and body experience. Each new task or deadline adds to your stress, resulting in an accumulation throughout the day. Stress levels can rise as suddenly as spotting your boss over the tops of the cubicles, hearing a phone ringing, or having an e-mail arrive.

Deadline pressure, fueled by organization climates and individual working styles (see Lesson 3, "The Toxic Workplace"), result in many people working longer hours. As you've undoubtedly witnessed, it's not unusual for people to work straight through their lunch breaks and on into the late evening to try to meet deadlines (all the while snacking at their desks). If the workplace is your main source of stress, the more time you find yourself in the office, the greater your need to minimize potential office stressors.

The Good and the Bad

As you learned in Lesson 1, "What Is Stress?" stress can be both motivating and detrimental.

PLAIN ENGLISH

> **Motivating stress**   Stress that stimulates and challenges you, as opposed to preventing you from accomplishing tasks.

Stress is necessary to your working energy level. Negative stress, however, often results from increased work pressure and may make you anxious and irritable. Stress in the workplace can come from many sources:

- A difficult boss or co-worker

- Lack of recognition

- Long hours

- Unclear expectations

- Lack of job security

- Multiple, complex tasks with deadlines

- Fluctuating expectations

TIP

> Dozens of other factors or combinations of factors may also prove stressful to you. A single cause of an individual's stress is hard to pinpoint. No matter what the source, it's important to work toward finding ways to keep the stress in balance.

STRESS AT YOUR DESK

At work or at home, stress is unhealthy for the body. It can cause a tightening of muscles, leading to muscle soreness. Affected muscles include those in the face, shoulders, and neck. This causes headaches in the back of the head, which spread from there. Working at a desk in front of PC tends to exacerbate the situation. As everyone who has ever had a headache knows, this makes it difficult to concentrate and focus on the task at hand.

TIP

> Time away from work should be just that—time away.

WHEN STRESS THREATENS YOUR PROFESSIONAL RELATIONSHIPS

It is vital to keep stress levels in check, because they can lead to job burnout. With burnout, you end up "down on yourself," detached from your work, and low on energy. A vicious cycle ensues: Becoming removed from your work and from the people you work with makes your working habits less productive.

PLAIN ENGLISH

Burnout   A specific type of stress that involves diminished personal accomplishment, depersonalization, and
emotional exhaustion.

If you fail to keep your stress levels in check, your relationships at the
office will be affected. Your co-workers will notice changes in your
attitude, your anxiety, and your emotions. These changes will serve to
isolate you from people. No one wants to spend time with someone
who is volatile.

CAUTION

Lashing out or blowing up at someone in the office
because of stress should be avoided at all costs. Even
one such incident can leave you with a reputation as an
unfriendly and dangerous person. Co-workers could have
a hard time approaching you, and you could end up
being isolated or outcast.

SIMPLE WAYS TO MAINTAIN BALANCE

You can do many simple things to maintain balance—many of which
require simple adjustments to what you already do:

- While at work, *move* more! You can relieve tension and soreness in muscles due to stress by flexing and relaxing your
  muscles periodically.

- Spend more time walking. If you tend to spend hours at your
  desk, stand up and walk around the room or just stretch in
  place at least every 20 minutes.

- If you consistently use an elevator, take the stairs every now
  and then.

TIP

Keeping stress levels in check creates a healthier personal working environment. If your stress levels are controlled, you have a better ability to focus, concentrate, and relax.

ELIMINATE UNNEEDED TASKS

In his book, *The Effective Executive,* management sage Dr. Peter Drucker tells us that 80 percent of what we do at work is dictated by habit and not by need. That means much of what you do during the workday is done because you always do things that way. Is it the best way, though? And does performing unnecessary tasks add to your workload and hence your stress level?

TIP

Ask yourself this question: "Does this need to be done at all?" This question often leads to greater focus, less time wasted on nonessential tasks, and less stress.

What kinds of tasks may not need to be done at all anymore? Try these on for size:

- Checking for e-mail messages three times a day when once a day is sufficient.

- Making a backup hard copy of documents on your disk.

- Sending a fax and then sending a follow-up letter containing the same information as the fax.

- Reviewing previous policies and procedures that have been replaced by newer ones.

- Reviewing training manuals and guides that have been replaced by newer ones.

ORDER CAN BRING RELIEF

When stress affects your concentration at work, a simple solution is to make a schedule. Scheduling not only allows you to plan and control your use of time, but also forces you to consider your priorities and goals.

Along with scheduling, set goals. Jotting down long-term and short-term goals in your weekly planner will keep you focused on your priorities rather than someone else's. Well-structured time and feelings of accomplishment when a goal is met will come as a direct result.

 TIP

You will use your time more effectively if you not only write down goals, but also write down the steps and activities required to meet those goals.

Taking time for yourself each week can also make time spent in the office more productive. Find a way to relax so that you can keep your perspective. Spend your lunch break outside, go for a massage, listen to a favorite CD all the way through, or engage in whatever it takes to clear your mind. Including a special break will leave you feeling more calm and focused at your work.

FACE YOUR SPACE

Along with organizing your time, organizing your space in a manner conducive to your work style is important. Don't let your desk become a mess of papers, mail, and sticky notes. In such cases, reminders are hard to find and can easily be overlooked, time is wasted looking for documents, and you have less space to work.

 TIP

Stay organized. The organization of your physical environment is as important as the organization of goals in your weekly planner. Filing cabinets, folders, and labeling systems can be wonderful tools—use them.

ENVISIONING CALM

If you absolutely can't get out of the office for a break, take a few minutes for some visualization (more on this in Lesson 11, "Visualization and Guided Imagery"). This technique focuses on creating a mental picture of something that cultivates a feeling of calm or simply makes you happy. If you need to, you can close your eyes to do this.

You can also use visualization to calm your fears of future events. If you fear a meeting with a certain person, for example, you can visualize the encounter going well before it happens.

BREATHE AND RECOUP

Another helpful strategy is to take a five- to ten-minute break to breathe (more on this in Lesson 12, "Breathing"). Find a *quiet* place. Close your eyes and focus all of your attention on taking deep, steady breaths. Like visualization, this technique allows you to pause and recenter yourself in the midst of your work. You will be surprised at what a calming effect this has.

When you return to your desk, you will find yourself with a better ability to concentrate.

THE QUEST FOR BALANCE

To maintain balance at work among otherwise stress-inducing events, remind yourself of the positive side of all situations. When a situation arises that you view as negative, pause momentarily to find the positive side of it.

 TIP

Stressful situations often are a matter of interpretation. If you have a hard time finding any positive attributes for a given situation at work, say to yourself, "It could be worse," and proceed from there. You will be surprised what a difference perception makes.

A simple source of balance for some people is keeping a plant in their office. Many small plants require minimal care and can flourish in an office setting.

TIP

Adding something living to your office to mingle among the abundance of inanimate objects can help liven up the atmosphere and lift your spirits.

It is also important to exercise your creativity. If the nature of your job does not lend itself to creative expression, find your own ways to express yourself. Even if it is something as simple as color-coding your daily planner, the use of colors is a good release and will contribute to relaxation.

MAKE YOUR TIME AWAY COUNT

Outside the office, prepare your mind and body for the time you spend in the office:

- **Eat a balanced diet.** Avoid heavy, carbohydrate-laden lunches/snacks. Eat more fruit and vegetable snacks. You'll have more energy and less internal discomfort.

- **Exercise.** If you work out a little every day or just a few days a week, you will notice a decrease in muscle tension, which will make your office chair much more comfortable. This time is important for you, so schedule it if necessary.

- **Build relationships.** Never underestimate the importance of time spent with friends. Your good friends have a way of calming you, whether you need someone to talk to, laugh with, or take a break with. Who else would listen to you vent about work?

- **Get enough sleep.** A well-rested body and mind are your best tools for higher performance. There is little at work that you can do well when you are groggy and tired.

Fortunately you have a variety of stress-management options in and out of the office, before work, after work, and during breaks. Using these options will increase your balance, allowing you to be more productive and making you an easier co-worker to be around.

The 30-Second Recap

- With an increase in the speed of communication and the continually changing marketplace, time pressure within the modern office environment equals increased stress.

- Although some stress might be motivating, over time, negative stress can harm individuals' working relationships and decrease their overall ability to work productively.

- With an awareness of stress's harmful effects, individuals can practice lifestyle changes and simple techniques to manage stress and maintain more balance in the workplace.

LESSON 5
Stress at Home

In this lesson, you learn about sources of household stress, tips for conflict management, and suggestions for dealing with specific household stresses.

SOURCES OF HOUSEHOLD STRESS

For many people, stress in the workplace is the least of their worries. In fact, studies conducted by the American Medical Association (AMA) show that family-related stress often has a stronger impact on people's health and well-being than other types of stress that get more press. Stress in the home comes from more than just family. There is also household management stress, or financial stress. Certain times of the year are also infamous for inducing stress, especially holidays.

CAUTION

> AMA studies show that people with high levels of family stress spend more time in doctors' offices, are referred to specialists more often, and are hospitalized more often.

Keeping domestic stresses in check is not only a key to improving quality of life, but also an important means of staying healthy.

COUPLEHOOD AND BLENDED FAMILIES

Some of the most prevalent household stressors are family relationships. Couples constantly face stress, and the most obvious source is when the relationship is in trouble. Household stress can wear on a marriage or partnership. When things don't work out and families experience separation and divorce, the result is even more stress for parents and children. As the following table indicates, a high divorce rate in society is a continuing fact.

Marriages and Divorces in the United States

Year	Marriages (in Millions)	Rate/1,000 pop. (Percent)	Divorces (in Millions)	Rate/1,000 pop. (Percent)
1990	2.443	9.8	1.182	4.7
1991	2.371	9.4	1.187	4.7
1992	2.362	9.3	1.215	4.8
1993	2.334	9.0	1.187	4.6
1994	2.362	9.1	1.191	4.6

Source: U.S. National Center for Health Statistics

Blended families often endure more household stresses than other families. More than one-third of all children in the United States become part of a stepfamily before the age of 18. These children have a higher risk of both behavioral and emotional problems, which can cause stress for the whole family.

CAUTION

Blended families can be a source of stress for all family members.

To reduce some of the stress, adults should discuss, *before* they marry, where they will live and how they will share their money. Sometimes buying a house together is better for everyone because it feels like a new beginning.

TIP

If you are remarrying, you should also discuss the role the stepparent will play in raising any children from previous relationships. This will eliminate confusion and possible stepping on toes that could put stress on the marriage.

Children are especially vulnerable to the stress created by blended families. Children are expected to adjust to a new environment and a new stepparent, while combating feelings of abandonment by the non-custodial parent. Children also will experience stress if they are put in the position of defending a parent if one speaks badly about the other. Therefore, it is important to keep their emotional needs in mind when you make decisions.

The following are pointers for parents to keep in mind:

- Stepparents should not rush a close relationship with their stepchildren.

- Avoid speaking against your ex-spouse in front of the children so they won't get defensive.

- Avoid putting the children in the middle by questioning whether your spouse is more loyal to you or them.

CAUTION

When parents remarry, often they don't maintain as much contact with their children, which can be damaging to the child's self-esteem.

MANAGING FINANCES

Keeping finances under control helps reduce stress in the home. Balance checkbooks regularly, and file receipts and bills away in an accessible place. Being in debt, whether it is credit cards or loans, causes stress for too many people. It is important to live within your means to avoid owing money you don't have (see Lesson 10, "The Time/Money/Stress Connection").

To deal with debt, you should eliminate nonessential spending. This can be done without cutting back in crucial areas like food and insurance. For example, you can dine at home, rather than eat out, or watch a video at home, instead of going out to the movies. Do this until you can pay off all your debts. When that is taken care of, start saving money.

TURKEY AND YULETIDE

The holiday season is another huge precipitator of stress in the household. It seems like holiday stress affects us all at some point. Most holiday stress happens when we put unrealistic expectations on ourselves and others because of an image we have of how the holiday season should be.

CAUTION

Many people expect to have the perfect holiday season, as portrayed in movies and on television. Be true to your own feelings and limits, and try to ignore the hype that focuses on what a "real" home should be like during the holidays.

People also feel obligated to buy too many gifts, or gifts that are too expensive for their budget. You will be less stressed if you can accept that it is better to stay within your spending limit.

TIP

Watch your spending at holiday time and resist the urge to use credit cards too much. This can lead to year-round financial stress, because the bills linger on until fully paid.

CAUTION

Holidays tend to magnify other existing stressors, such as family illnesses, tragic losses, and relatives who you don't get along with. The key to keeping stress levels in check is, again, being true to yourself. Do not expect the holidays to be a magical time when problems disappear. The idea is not to turn into a scrooge but to simply be realistic. Know what you can do with the resources you have.

TIPS FOR CONFLICT MANAGEMENT

Much of the domestic stress that people experience comes from arguments among family members. So let's focus on conflict management.

PLAIN ENGLISH

Conflict management   Strategies for resolving sharp disagreements, of interests or ideas, or emotional disturbances.

Arguments can be highly disruptive not only to the individuals involved, but also to other members of the family who might feel obligated to choose sides or play mediator. Whether the conflict is a minor difference or a full-blown argument, methods of conflict resolution can reduce the stress it causes.

All relationships have conflict. Its existence is actually a healthy sign. The part that can be unhealthy is how you handle the conflict.

Unhealthy management styles include …

- Denying that there is a problem.
- Giving in just to avoid a conflict.
- Blaming others.
- Using power to get one's way.

Many of these approaches only prolong the problem, because they never solve it entirely. As a result, the problem festers and generally resurfaces in another form.

WIN-WIN SOLUTIONS

It is important to enter any conflict with the right frame of mind. Never lose sight of the relationship you have with that person. If you feel like you might say something you'll regret, take the time to cool off. When you approach any conflict with a negative attitude, you can expect trouble.

Healthy solutions to conflicts means everybody wins. This is possible when a conflict has more than two alternatives, which it often does. You might have one solution in mind while your adversary has another. If you don't like each other's choices, there might be an alternative solution that you can mutually devise to suit both parties.

COMPROMISES

Another healthy solution, instead of everyone winning, is having no one lose. When you arrive at a point where neither person likes the other person's choice, you again try to come up with an alternate solution, but there might not be one that you both like. You might have to put up with some things that you don't like, but so will the other person.

PLAIN ENGLISH

Compromise   A settlement in which both sides make concessions, or a solution that is midway between two alternatives.

TIP

In this case, try to find a solution that you can both at least live with. In other words, a solution that is more of a compromise.

TAKING TURNS

When neither of the two earlier approaches works, or when a problem has only two, polar solutions and you can't bridge the gap, take turns. In this situation, only one person gets his way, for now. Next time, the other person gets *his* way. This win-lose, lose-win approach diminishes the impact of the losses, because the losing party knows that, next time, he will win.

Both parties should try to be respectful and have the other person's interests in mind. Other people want to have their chance to be heard

as much as you do. Don't always feel like you have to win. A dis-
agreement should not turn into a competition, and if it feels that way,
you and the other person are more likely to get defensive.

CAUTION

Sometimes it is hard to see any other side but yours, but
you have to try to understand the other person's side.

Caring Counts

When the person you are in conflict with is someone you care about, you
must be willing to give and receive apologies. Inevitably, there will be
times when you or someone else involved gets hurt or upset. Apologies
can help speed up the healing process, and so can declarations of love.

TIP

Even during disagreements, it is helpful to be able to
say "I love you" or "I care for you."

Becoming More Aware

Practicing basic conflict management skills will reduce some household stress. However, other techniques can help, too. Become aware of
what stressors affect you, and notice your reactions to those stressors.

TIP

Don't ignore your domestic stress. Determine specifically
what causes you stress in the home and how your body
responds to the stress. Notice if you become nervous or
physically upset. Then examine what you're telling yourself about the meaning of these things. Are they worth
anguish?

GRANT ME THE SERENITY

Be aware of what you can and cannot change. Perhaps you can work on avoiding your stressors, eliminating them completely, or reducing the intensity of their influence.

TIP

> Shorten your exposure to stressors by taking a break or getting away, using the time to relax and gain new perspective.

Learn to reduce the intensity of your emotional reactions to potential stress. As discussed in Lesson 2, "How Does Stress Show Up?" stress reactions are triggered by your body's perception of danger. By keeping your perspective in check, you can avoid viewing your stressors in an exaggerated way.

TIP

> You can't always please everyone, and most issues are not urgent.

If you can put each situation in perspective, you will be able to recognize your excess emotions and understand the stressor as something you can deal with.

PHYSICAL RESERVES

You can also learn to moderate your physical reactions to stress. Taking slow, deep breaths will bring your heart rate down and your respiration back to normal. A variety of relaxation techniques can reduce muscle tension (more on this in Lesson 12, "Breathing").

CAUTION

> Numerous medications can assist you, but learning to moderate these stress reactions in natural ways is a more effective long-term solution.

Building up your physical reserves will better prepare you to face everyday household stresses. Moderate exercise and a well-balanced diet are extremely important. Getting enough sleep and being consistent with your sleep schedule are also important. Avoid nicotine, excessive caffeine, and other stimulants.

TIP

> If you maintain a healthy, conditioned body, potentially stressful situations won't hit you as hard.

EMOTIONAL RESERVES

Emotional reserves are as important as physical reserves for handling potential household stressors. Maintain healthy friendships and relationships.

TIP

> A good support network can help you put things in perspective when you can't do it alone or when you need an outside opinion.

Most important, be a friend to yourself. Expect some frustrations, failures, and sorrows—and take them gracefully. Don't be hard on yourself. You have to be willing to be human.

THE 30-SECOND RECAP

- Stress in the home results from many factors, including family relationships, finances, and how one approaches the holidays.

- Healthy conflict resolution solves family disagreements and arguments, helping relieve household stress.

- Keeping a level head and being aware of your limits can help you deal with stress in the home.

- Strive to be a friend to yourself, recognizing that frustrations, failures, and sorrows are part of every life. Take them with as much grace as you can muster.

LESSON 6
Getting Sleep, Staying in Balance

In this lesson, you learn the importance of keeping your life in balance by getting proper sleep, avoiding overwork, and recognizing when you could be overcontrolling.

THERE IS NO SUBSTITUTE FOR GOOD SLEEP

Keeping your life stress-free and in balance is highly desirable, yet as we've seen, there are forces throughout society conspiring to ensure that you remain in any state other than balanced. With each passing month, more things compete for your time and attention. Take the time now to carve out a pattern that fits the way you work and the way you want to live. The lessons you've completed so far will aid you greatly, but the need for sleep cannot be denied.

NAME THAT EVENT

A momentous event occurred in 1878. Can you guess what it is? Before telling you the answer, here are some clues. Prior to that time, the typical person slept anywhere from nine to eleven hours a night. People usually retired within an hour or two of the sun going down and rose at sunrise.

After 1878, within a few short years, the average amount of sleep per adult fell from around ten hours per night to eight. Since then it has fallen even more, hovering just above seven hours.

What happened in 1878? Give up? Thomas Edison invented the light bulb.

TIP

It is an anthropological phenomenon to fall asleep when
it is dark and wake up when it is light.

Artificial light via the light bulb, as well as all the other inventions that
followed, dramatically shifted our sleeping patterns. Yet for tens of
thousands of years, humans slept an average of 10 hours a night and
more. Is it possible that human physiology could change in the course
of 10 or 12 decades? Not likely. If you're getting 8 hours of very good
sleep a night, you still may not get all the rest your body requires.

TIP

Be generous with yourself when it comes to sleep. Give
yourself rest when your body feels the need for it. Proper
sleep is one of the best stress inhibitors available.

HARD-FOUGHT GAINS

Your quest for more sleep will not come without its battles. In the
United States, people have added 158 hours to their annual work and
commuting time since three decades ago. The rest of the world is
beginning to catch up!

CAUTION

Without adequate sleep, you cannot possibly perform
your best work—no matter how well you have lulled
yourself into believing otherwise.

Studies of Japanese workers who put in inordinately long days reveal
that instead of increasing overall productivity, after a given number of
hours, productivity actually declined. After a few more hours, these
workers actually became counterproductive—they started to make
errors that undid the previous good work they had done.

TIP

> The amount of sleep you need on a regular basis is
> something only you can determine. Everyone differs in
> this category, and there is no point in comparing your-
> self to others.

Don't believe the reports of others. With great bravado, people routinely announce in offices that they got by with three or four hours of
sleep last night, that they average five hours a night, that they routinely get to bed at two a.m., or that "I was up the entire night." Such
statements only further the propagation of myths around sleep.

CAUTION

> Everyone needs good sleep on a regular basis. In tests of
> those who claimed to be able to get by on less sleep,
> very few exhibited the ability to do so.

THE SIGNS ARE HIGHLY VISIBLE

Inadequate sleep leads to a variety of undesirable results:

- You become less aware.

- You constantly feel worn out.

- Your immune system is weakened.

On top of this, combined with too little sleep, any illness you do contract will be more severe.

If you feel tired day after day, that is indication enough that you need
more sleep. If any of the following are evident, you need to get to bed
immediately, because you are taking chances with your health, and
potentially the well-being of others:

- **Lack of appetite or indigestion**   You may be a chow hound
  from way back, but if you have trouble when it comes to

mealtimes, particularly trouble swallowing, sleep deprivation may be at the root.

- **Fatigue in the morning even after a full night's sleep** Sleep experts agree that, if people are otherwise healthy, there is little reason for them to be less than chipper following a full night of sleep. If you find yourself wanting to nod off at 10:00 or 11:00 in the morning, it is time to pay attention to your body's signal.

- **Loss of libido**   If you are not as interested in sex as you used to be, it is probably not your age that is the cause, but rather your lack of sleep. This generally occurs gradually enough as to be unnoticeable by you but is entirely of concern to your partner.

- **Prolonged fatigue**   If you feel out of sorts following several nights of full sleep, chances are that you have gone too long getting far too little sleep prior to those recent nights. Embark on a course right now of getting at least eight hours of uninterrupted sleep and taking some extra time on the weekends.

- **Annoyance with minor tasks**   If you have trouble adding up numbers, don't want to field phone calls, and find yourself avoiding tasks that previously represented no real challenge, chances are you may not have the rest you need and hence the mental clarity to proceed with these tasks.

- **Red eyes**   If your eyes are red, and you didn't just arrive from the West coast on a late-night flight, you've had too little sleep. The condition of your eyes is one of the clearest indications of too little sleep.

Having too little sleep can contribute to diminished joy in life. Everything seems so blasé. Stress is predictable. On top of that, you can be a danger to others.

CAUTION

> If you suffer from sleeplessness and work in a situation where you operate equipment, your health and safety, as well as that of those around you, can be in jeopardy. If you operate a motor vehicle, you may be gambling with your life, the lives of fellow passengers, and the lives of others on the road.

THE MICROSLEEP PHENOMENA

Martin Moore-Ede, Ph.D., in his book *The Twenty-Four Hour Society,* observes that too many people unknowingly engage in *microsleep.* Occurrences of microsleep are 10- to 15-second bouts of sleep that occur in the middle of the day while the person otherwise appears to be fully functional. For example, the following all represent times at which microsleep occurs:

- Office professionals engage in microsleep right at their desks, which is not particularly harmful to the people around them.

- Parents engage in microsleep while driving their children to and from lessons.

- Vanpool drivers engage in microsleep while transporting six or eight people.

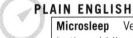
PLAIN ENGLISH

> **Microsleep**   Very brief, nondiscernable sleep episodes in the middle of the day.

The danger is obvious. Think about your own sleep pattern over the last week, month, and year. Have you been chronically depriving yourself of sleep? Could you be among those who engage in microsleep? The possibility is more distinct than you might have thought.

UNFAIR TO YOURSELF AND TO YOUR EMPLOYER

If you arrive at work exhausted, you can't possibly be as efficient as you would be otherwise. In many respects, you are gypping your employer. Presumably your organization hired the full and complete you, which you are not able to offer if you continually arrive in less than your best condition.

To ensure that you get proper sleep, you need to be comfortable in your bedroom. The climate and atmosphere should be right for you and your mate. If possible, once you get to sleep, you need to stay asleep until you have to get up. If you're not comfortable, you won't sleep well.

The following are suggestions for making your bedroom more comfortable:

- Keeping your bedroom slightly cool will help you and your mate sleep better. It seems like one person is always hot while the other person is always cold. Bring out the extra blankets for the cold one so both of you can be happy.

- Don't be jostled out of a deep sleep by the telephone ringing. Whether it's an important call, misdial, or a prank, once your sleeping pattern has been disrupted for the night, you may not have the same benefits of a full night's sleep. Turn the ringer off before you go to bed or have the calls rerouted to an answering machine or service. This tip goes for pagers, also!

- Eliminate distractions in the bedroom. You may be more comfortable falling asleep with the television on, especially if you live by yourself, but most likely the television will wake you up in the middle of the night with the volume seemingly a lot louder than it was when you went to sleep.

- Keep pets from jumping up and down on your bed and running around your house all night.

CAUTION

> Even if you have a TV that turns off automatically, the extra time you spend in bed watching it until it goes off will have an accumulated de-energizing effect.

- If you need the alarm clock to wake up in the morning, make sure you get up the first time it goes off. If you hit the snooze button and fall back to sleep, you're doing yourself more harm than good. You won't fully get back to sleep before the alarm clock goes off again, which disrupts your sleeping and makes you feel worse than if you had just gotten up to begin with.

- Allow yourself enough room to move while sleeping. Make sure you have a bed sufficiently large enough to allow you and your partner freedom of movement. Fear of bumping into one another will restrict your movements and unknowingly diminish the quality of your sleep.

- Avoid caffeine for at least six hours before retiring, and avoid alcohol altogether if you're interested in having a good sleep that night. Alcohol disrupts the sleep. You'll fall asleep quickly, but you'll wake up too early. Then you're likely to have trouble getting back to sleep.

Finally, go to sleep when you're tired, not because the clock happens to say a particular time. When you ignore the message your body is giving you, you pay a price.

Is Lack of Sleep Diminishing Your Staff's Effectiveness?

What if one of your key stressors is the lack of alertness or productivity you observe in your staff? If you supervise others (see Lesson 3, "The Toxic Workplace"), how often have you looked out across your office or plant floor and seen employees dragging their tails, even at midmorning?

Here is data that may prompt you to explore innovative ways to tackle one of the most pervasive problems in society: an *exhausted* workforce. In a survey conducted by the National Sleep Foundation, 51 percent of the American workforce reports that sleepiness on the job interferes with the amount of work they get done. Forty percent of employees admit that the quality of their work suffers when they are sleepy, and nearly one out of five (19 percent) report making occasional or frequent work errors due to sleepiness.

CAUTION

While sleep experts recommend at least eight hours of sleep a night in order to function properly, one-third of American adults (33 percent) sleep only six and one-half hours or less nightly during the work week.

PLAIN ENGLISH

Exhaustion   The state of being used up, tired out, or completely emptied or drained. Many adults experience exhaustion because of a lack of adequate sleep.

Is it any wonder that some of the people you supervise are consistently less productive than they could be? One out of four adults has difficulty getting up for work two or more days per week, and 27 percent of adults say they are sleepy at work two or more days a week. At least two-thirds of adults report that sleepiness makes concentrating (68 percent) and *handling stress* (66 percent) on the job more difficult.

As if this data weren't bad enough, 58 percent say that making decisions and solving problems are more difficult when they are sleepy. Listening to co-workers is more difficult when sleepy, according to 57 percent of respondents. Overall, employees estimate that the quality and quantity of their work is diminished by about 30 percent when they are sleepy.

CAUTION

> Sleep deprivation is a serious issue for supervisors and entrepreneurs running their own ventures. At risk is productivity and safety, as well as employment longevity.

Innovations Needed!

To retain and get the best of your staff calls for innovative measures. Here are some possibilities:

- Encourage employees to take quick naps at their desks.

- Send employees home early (without reprimand) when their need for sleep is apparent.

- Encourage employees to maintain sleep logs.

- Establish nap rooms.

It's far better to encourage naps than to have employees pretend to be alert.

We've got a lot to do in this world, and we each have the greatest chance of being at our best when we're well-rested!

The 30-Second Recap

- Getting good sleep night after night is the primary prerequisite for being productive in your job and keeping your stress levels in check.

- The amount of sleep you need on a regular and continual basis is unique and highly personal.

- It is easy to determine how much sleep you require—if you pay attention, your body will tell you.

- Devise a strategy to ensure that you get the amount of sleep you need to feel rested, awake, and alert in the morning.

LESSON 7
Curbing Procrastination

In this lesson, you learn ways to prevent procrastination and its associated stress so that you'll be better able to accomplish overwhelming and unpleasant tasks with relative ease.

PROCRASTINATION AND STRESS

Whenever you let low-priority tasks get in the way of higher priority tasks, you are *procrastinating*.

PLAIN ENGLISH

Procrastination   To put off doing a task, to delay an activity or task, or to ignore something that demands your attention.

Putting things off inevitably leads to a pile-up—too much to do and not enough time to do it. Whether you procrastinate at home or in the office, the demands it puts on your time cause stress.

CAUTION

Your stress level increases as minor tasks pile up and begin to seem larger than they really are.

PLEASANT TASKS ARE NOT THE PROBLEM

Things that are enjoyable to you are usually not the problem. You get those tasks done with relative ease. The problem comes when you perceive a task as difficult, inconvenient, or scary. This is when you are likely to shift into procrastination mode.

People often fool themselves by saying things like, "I work better under pressure, so I don't need to do this now," or "I'll wait until I'm in the mood to do it." Statements like these help us convince ourselves to procrastinate, which causes unnecessary stress.

SMALL TASKS MOUNT UP

Suppose you have several tasks before you, each of which would take only five to ten minutes to complete. Any one of these tasks would be no big deal to tackle. The thought of handling all of them, however, becomes daunting.

As the list of things you need to take care of grows, and you feel yourself getting somewhat behind, all those tasks start to loom even larger! There are many ways to break through procrastination and reduce the stress that it causes.

FIRST, GET ORGANIZED

When you "divide and conquer," you have a good chance of overcoming procrastination. Regard each task before you as a distinct entity. If you have a large job, break it down into individual tasks, each regarded as separate. When you tackle a five-minute job and gain the satisfaction of having completed it, you have more energy, focus, and direction for another five-minute job.

Likewise, if you do five 5-minute jobs, with each job you feel a sense of victory—however minor—and you're spurred on to the next job, and the next. In this manner, five 5-minute jobs can actually be easier to complete than one 25-minute job.

TIP

On my way to writing 27 books, I saw each chapter as a distinct task in and of itself, completely apart from the book.

When completing this chapter, for example, I got up, stretched, walked around, took a big drink of water, and forgot all about what's next. Then as I approached Lesson 8, "The Stress of Information Overload," I gave it my full energy and attention. By approaching each of the lessons in this book as individual tasks, the daunting project of writing an under 200-page book in a very short time didn't seem so bad.

TIP

> If I had to write an entire manuscript with no individual lessons in it (in other words, if the book were one huge lesson), it would be a far more difficult task. Why? No ability to divide and conquer.

CLEAR YOUR DESK

Simply having too much in your visual field can be an impediment to getting started. When you have one project or one task at hand, your odds of maintaining clarity and focus increase dramatically. This works even better if you're not in your own office but at a conference table or at some other post where you have only the project materials at hand.

IDENTIFY THE REAL ISSUE

Sometimes you can't get started on something because you haven't identified some lingering issues that are affecting your feelings:

- Perhaps you're ambivalent about the task.

- Perhaps you think it's unnecessary or unworthy of you.

- Perhaps you resent doing it—for example, you weren't able to say no in the first place, and now you have to make good on your earlier promise.

Whatever the reason, when you identify some of the causes behind procrastination, you have a much better chance of getting past those barricades and getting started.

ELIMINATE DISTRACTIONS

Sometimes the reason you procrastinate on a project is because you fear you will be interrupted. To eliminate this possibility, eliminate distraction. Tell your receptionist to hold all calls. Turn off the ringer on your phone. Don't check your e-mail. Do whatever it takes to give yourself an uninterrupted span of time.

TIP

> If you think the task will take an hour, make sure that you don't have distractions for at least 90 minutes. Then, if you finish some time between 30 and 90 minutes later, you can always reenter "the world" when you choose.

PROCEEDING WITHOUT PAIN

Look for an "easy win." For whatever you're trying to tackle, find some element of it that you can complete quickly and easily and get an easy win. That's a far better method of getting started than tackling some difficult portion of it first.

TIP

> Suppose you're facing a difficult project. How could you get an easy win right off the bat? Open the file folder, scan the contents, and look for an easy entry point, some aspect of the project you can tackle now.

Sometimes simply organizing materials, putting them into smaller file folders, stapling items, or rearranging the order of things represents a good, easy win. Now at least you have a better handle on the project, the supporting items are arranged according to importance, and the probability of your continuing is reasonably assured.

CAUTION

Be careful. Too much rearrangement and organizing is a classic procrastination technique. Do not dwell on smaller, lower priority tasks. Use them as stepping stones.

REFRAME THE TASK

When novelist Tom Wolfe was working for *Esquire* magazine and was already past the deadline on an article, his editor gave him a wonderful suggestion. Wolfe was to start writing a letter to the editor, describing how he would approach the article and what he would put in it.

So Wolfe submitted a draft that started off like a letter. Sure enough, by eliminating the first paragraph or two and retaining the body of what Wolfe had written, the editor had the requisite material. The editor had simply *reframed* the task so that Wolfe could get started.

PLAIN ENGLISH

Reframe   To restructure so as to allow a different perspective.

TIP

Wolfe didn't have trouble writing the article; he simply had trouble getting started. By converting the notion of the assignment to a letter, the block was gone.

GIVE IT FIVE MINUTES

Suppose you don't want to tackle something now but know eventually you're going to have to start it. One way to get yourself immersed in it, kind of like dabbling your feet in a wading pool, is to devote five minutes of your attention to the task. At the end of five minutes, you may stop.

TIP

> Most people who use this five-minute approach don't want to stop after the fifth minute. A body, or a mind for that matter, tends to keep progressing in the same direction. If you've been on a project for five minutes, there is no reason why the sixth or seventh minute should be any more trying.

JUMP-STARTING

Sometimes the mere gesture of turning on your computer, popping a video into the VCR, or flipping on your pocket dictator is enough to get started on a task that you have been putting off. In essence, flipping on the switch to your PC, having it boot up, and perhaps taking it to the appropriate folder and file is analogous to jump-starting your car.

Suppose your car conks out on the side of the road, and your battery gets a jump-start. All of a sudden, the engine is revving—this is certainly not the time to turn off the car. You want to keep it on for a good 20 minutes. Likewise, once that PC boots up and your hard drive is humming, you may experience a jump-start in your ability to dive into the project.

USE TRADEOFFS

If you face many things competing for your attention (and who doesn't?), trade one project off against another.

Here's how it works: Suppose you have to do project A, and you've been putting it off. Along comes project B, which is more difficult, more involved, much scarier. Suddenly project A doesn't look so bad. Now tackle A headlong. You'll still have B to deal with, and that may keep you humming along on A!

GO COLD TURKEY

This is not recommended for everyone, and certainly not every time. Sometimes the only way to get started on a task is to dive into it headlong, cold turkey, not allowing yourself the opportunity to stray.

Surprisingly, when you practice the cold-turkey approach to procrastination, it's not nearly as upsetting as it sounds. In fact, it can be a great relief.

My friend Jim Cathcart, a fellow professional speaker, made the decision a few years back to chuck all of his hard-copy slides *en masse,* so that he would be forced to learn presentation software and convert his audiovisuals to the newer, more powerful media.

SEEKING HELP FROM OTHERS

Suppose that no matter what you try, you still can't get started on the task you've been putting off, and the associated stress is mounting. In that case, get a little help from your friends.

HAVE SOMEONE HOLD RANSOM MONEY

Suppose you want to accomplish something and you've been putting it off for weeks on end. You give a friend $500 and tell him or her, "If I don't finish this task by next Thursday, you get to keep the $500. (This approach is not for the meek or the broke.)

TIP

If $500 isn't enough to do the trick, make it $1,000 or $2,000. When you find the right sum, I guarantee you'll finish the task on time.

AFFILIATE

Some tasks are too challenging—you can't face them alone. Is somebody else trying to accomplish the same task you've been putting off? If so, you have a perfect partner or *affiliate* with whom to join forces.

PLAIN ENGLISH

Affiliate   An associate who has the same interests or goals that you have.

As you learned in Lesson 2, "How Does Stress Show Up?" whenever you can find someone who's up against the same challenges you are, you have the increased potential to achieve your goal.

REPORT TO SOMEBODY

One of the reasons you don't procrastinate at work as often as you might at home is that at work you generally report to a boss who is waiting for the results of your efforts and who pays you based on your efforts. If you don't complete your work, identifiable penalties will ensue.

 TIP

> If you have somebody waiting for your results, or waiting to hear about your progress, you significantly increase your ability to get started and to stay with the task at hand.

Although you don't necessarily want to treat personal tasks like assigned tasks, having to report your progress to someone increases your odds of starting and finishing in a timely manner. Even though this person isn't paying you, you're completing the task based on personal pride.

DELEGATE

Is there a portion of the task you can delegate? Particularly the part you don't like to do or are not good at doing?

Let's face it: There are some tasks that no matter how hard you try, how many lessons you take, and how long you practice, you're not going to be good at. But someone else will be good at them. Delegate the tasks to that person.

If you don't have the luxury of being able to delegate, maybe you can swap tasks. In return, take over what the other person doesn't want to do or isn't good at.

TIP

> Some people will never be good at playing the piano, some will never be good at programming, and some will never be good at creative writing. This is simply human nature. If you want to "nurture your nature," as Jim Cathcart says in his book, *The Acorn Principle,* capitalize on your strengths and shore up your weaknesses by getting help.

FIND A GUIDE

Is there someone in your office or the organization who can talk to you for five or ten minutes to get you started when procrastination is holding you back?

Particularly for tasks that seem overwhelming, if you can find someone knowledgeable about the situation who can give you a running start, ask that person to do so. After that person leaves, keep going on that task.

WAYS TO HELP YOURSELF

If you're facing an unpleasant task, it makes sense to follow it up with something you enjoy doing. In other words, you don't get to do what you enjoy until you do the unpleasant task.

TIP

> In his book *Bringing Out the Best in People,* Dr. Aubrey Daniels calls arranging an award following a good performance the "grandma principle." As grandma would say, you don't get to eat your ice cream until you eat your spinach.

GOT REST?

Half the time you can't get started on something because you are fatigued (see Lesson 6, "Getting Sleep, Staying in Balance"). When you're well-rested and well-nourished, you have the greatest chance of doing your best work. Conversely, when you don't have enough sleep and haven't eaten well, even the simplest of tasks can loom larger than it really is.

BARRICADE YOURSELF

Sometimes it makes sense to simply hole up somewhere so you can give your full attention to the task at hand.

Instead of going in to work, maybe you can work at home one day. Maybe you need to go to a hotel room. The point is to get yourself totally away from others so that no one can reach or find you, so that you have the opportunity to give your full attention to what you want to accomplish. When you're done, you'll find that your stress about it is vanquished!

THE 30-SECOND RECAP

- Identifying in vivid terms the consequences of not getting started and not accomplishing what you want to accomplish may be a sufficient incentive for you to get started.

- At any time, for any task, if you have trouble getting started, you have a variety of techniques to draw on to get you over the hurdle.

- Not all techniques work for all people, and no technique will necessarily work for any individual all the time. Try as many as necessary until you successfully get rolling.

LESSON 8
The Stress of Information Overload

In this lesson, you learn techniques for more effectively managing the information that overloads you on a daily basis.

I'M OVERWHELMED BY INFORMATION, THEREFORE I AM

The amount of information that you ingest to further your career can be staggering when you add it all up. In the course of a week, you may find yourself reading anywhere from 10 to 20 hours. In the information-packed society we all face today, information intake, largely in the form of reading, has undoubtedly become a major issue for you.

BASIC READING TECHNIQUES

Fortunately you can employ a variety of techniques to help get through your reading in record time, retaining what information you need to retain, and still feeling as if you have a life.

By *skimming*, you quickly find out whether you should read the article or chapter in greater depth. Often, skimming the first sentence or two is all you need to gain the essence of the information being provided.

PLAIN ENGLISH

Skimming Reading only the first few sentences of each paragraph in an article in a magazine, on the Web, or in a chapter in a book.

Scanning allows you to review a greater amount of material. If you encounter a large book or report, it is not often practical to skim. Using the scanning technique, you can learn enough about the book or document to determine whether it merits greater attention.

PLAIN ENGLISH

> **Scanning** Reviewing lists, charts, or exhibits in a book, an index, a table of contents, some of the chapter leads, and an occasional paragraph.

TIP

> Often, through scanning, you can identify the handful of relevant passages or pages worth photocopying, and then just recycle the book or report. (If you are concerned about the legality of photocopying, remember that if it is for limited personal use, you are not violating any copyright laws.)

EVALUATING THE SOURCE

Rather than plow through dozens of industry journals or Web sites, pick the best two or three, extracting or downloading articles of importance. Then you've cut down on the total volume you are exposed to, while relatively assuring that you're being exposed to the best and latest of what's going on in your industry or profession.

TIP

> The best sources are "the best" because they routinely provide the best information.

ASSEMBLING YOUR TOOLS

If you use a stick-em pad, paper clips, felt-tip pens, magic markers, scissors, and the like when you read hardcopy items, be sure to have them nearby.

When you extract or highlight information, you reduce your reading burden. Organize your information by maintaining a lean, mean file consisting of the material you're most likely to act upon.

CUTTING BOOKS DOWN TO SIZE

Many professionals lament the lack of opportunity to tackle some of the current longer, nonfiction books available. Amazon.com and BarnesandNoble.com make it abundantly clear just how many new books are out there. An article or slim report is one thing, but a 280- or 300-page book is a whole 'nother story.

 TIP

> As the Internet economy advances, much of what we know about management, product distribution, marketing, and customer service will change dramatically as a result of e-business opportunities.

Unquestionably there will be longer books you will want to read. Here are some ideas for getting through them in a highly productive manner:

- First, read the back jacket in detail. Here you will see what others have said about the book. This may prompt you to make a more concerted effort once you actually get inside.

- Also read the inside flaps. This material is usually written by the author but is presented as if written by the publisher. This is what the author wants you to know about the book and about him- or herself.

- Read the foreword to the book, if there is one. A friend of the author who is saying things about the author and the book that the author wanted to have said usually writes the foreword. A well-written foreword often serves as an "executive summary" to the entire book. It also often gives some insights as to the author's slant or bias.

- Read the table of contents. There may be some chapters that you decide to read immediately. Likewise, there may be other chapters that you determine you can safely skip.

- Read the introduction, usually written by the author and also providing an executive summary of sorts.

TIP

As you proceed to the chapters you have decided are most worth your attention, read at least the first two paragraphs. This will often tell you if you want to read the rest of the chapter. For those chapters where you don't want to continue, the first two paragraphs will usually at least give you a reasonable idea of what was covered.

- Go to the last page of each chapter and read either the last paragraph, any summary, or highlights list that is presented. These can be invaluable and, in some cases, serve as a substitute for reading the entire book.

- Review any resource lists, reference lists, charts, or graphs that strike your fancy as you flip through the book. When you are trying to save time, such features can be worthwhile.

- Go to the last chapter and read the last two or three pages. The author's major conclusions and observations are usually presented here. This will save you from reading at least the last chapter, possibly the last section of the book, and possibly the entire book.

- Always, always, always photocopy the handful of key pages you believe will have future value for you.

READING ON THE RUN

A two- or three-page article can easily be folded and kept in your pocket. The next time you're stuck in any kind of line, pull out the article and read for a couple of minutes. You won't feel much stress or anxiety for having to wait in line, because you're being productive. Sometimes you'll finish the whole article. Sometimes you'll hardly get started, when you find yourself at the head of the line. No problem—put the article back in your pocket for the next line.

TIP

> Pull out your article on the bus, train, plane, or taxi ride.

Don't take a ton of reading material with you when you're traveling for business, because you inevitably end up creating more stress and more tasks for yourself that you can't fully act upon when you are on the road.

TIP

> Do take the thin files representing the few key articles and few key pages you want to get to. This is easy to handle and will only get lighter as you chuck the pages you no longer need.

If you have a lot of reading to do, sometimes it is more effective and easier mentally to mix some of the longer, involved articles with the shorter, easier ones. By alternating back and forth between the complex and the simple, you continue to mow down the pile without taxing your intellect too much.

GET THEE TO A QUIET PLACE

Obviously, the quieter the place where you read, the faster and easier you will be able to get through the pile. Yet, if you have some familiarity with what you are reading, even a somewhat noisy place can be a sufficient environment. Find a quiet sanctuary whenever you are reading the following:

- Highly technical issues

- Items with which you have little familiarity

- Heavily philosophical or think pieces

- Anything that requires you to pause and reflect before proceeding.

It is just too difficult to do this kind of reading when surrounded by distractions. In any case, make it part of your reading task to find the place where you personally find it most conducive to tackle the subject matter at hand.

TIP

> Undoubtedly you know the value of reading early in the morning before others come into your office, or before you have left your house. The same holds true for the evening, after everyone has left the office, or at home, after everyone else has retired.

Anytime you find yourself unable to sleep, particularly for more than a 30-minute stretch, fill in the time with reading. Sleep specialists say that reading is a worthwhile technique to engage in until you feel drowsy again and can nod off.

LESSENING YOUR TASK

When you suspect that a subscription is perhaps still worth the money but not worth your time, let it go with the last issue. If you don't miss it, you are ahead of the game. If you do miss it, the publication will take you back, often at a reduced rate. Perhaps you can gain the same information online, or visit the library periodically and peruse three or four issues of the same publication at high speed.

TIP

> Anytime you come across a review of a book, an excerpt, a critique, or anything else that gives you the essence of what the book says, you are ahead of the game.

TIP

> Many libraries stock books and lectures on tape—and, in most cases, abridged versions.

You can safely listen to a cassette as you drive (an entirely different activity than talking on a cell phone, which actively competes for the attention crucial to safe driving). This is a relatively easy way to gain information, avoid eyestrain, and still arrive on time.

NEWSLETTERS HELP ENORMOUSLY

By scanning a couple of newsletter directories in the reference section of your library, you can determine the key newsletters in your industry or profession. The *Oxbridge Directory of Newsletters, The Newsletter Yearbook,* and *National Trade and Professional Organization* each gives information about key newsletters that are available for a fee or for free.

TIP

> Newsletters cut down on your overall reading time. Their implied mission is to supply you with succinct, well-crafted, critical information so that you don't have to round it up yourself.

With the plethora of online 'zines, you can achieve the same results without leaving your desk. Be wary of surfing the Web aimlessly because the infinite labyrinth of information out there will consume your life if you let it!

TIP

> BarCharts at www.barcharts.com and Permachart Quick Reference Guides at www.cram.com offer well-constructed, full-color, information-laden, laminated charts on a variety of computer, academic, health, and business topics. The charts are illustrated, lightweight, durable, and a marvel to behold.

THE 30-SECOND RECAP

- Skimming the first sentence or two of each paragraph of an article, and scanning a book's table of contents for selected chapters, are two highly effective ways to get through massive amounts of reading material.

- Don't take too much reading material with you when you're traveling for business.

- Do take the thin files representing the few key articles and pages you want to read.

- Invest in any online service, newsletter, or briefing service that succinctly captures the essence of important issues in your industry.

LESSON 9

Taking the Stress Out of Travel

In this lesson, you learn ways to manage stress while traveling, including organizational tips and ideas for relieving stress on the road.

ATTITUDE ADJUSTMENT

If you've traveled anywhere lately, particularly by air, you don't need a lecture on how hectic travel has become. More people are traveling to more places than ever before. The travel industry hasn't caught up, or apparently woken up, to the fact that yesterday's level of service is no longer sufficient. Often your challenge as an individual traveler is making the journey from point A to point B with the least amount of stress.

A key to reducing travel stress is simply maintaining a positive attitude. Much of the stress of travel results from encountering new things and experiencing situations beyond our control. Most people are accustomed to having a large degree of control over situations in their daily life. Frustrating as it may be, even with perfect planning, traveling is one of the activities we often cannot control.

TIP

If you can step back and evaluate your attitude, you likely can curb many of the emotional responses that lead to travel stress. It is your option to control the way you experience a situation. Relax and focus on maintaining your perspective and a positive attitude.

GETTING ORGANIZED IS THE KEY

Getting organized and establishing systems (much as you do in the workplace) is fundamental to traveling with less stress. For example, long before your next trip, make yourself a packing list and keep it in a file on your computer. Print it every time you pack for a trip, and you save yourself a lot of time and energy.

TIP

> For some trips, not all items on your list need to be printed because you won't be taking them. So print a modified, *shorter* list.

Personal organization expert Barbara Hemphill advises making a box next to each item and checking it off as it is packed. Here are her suggestions, clothing and personal items excluded:

Basics:

- ❑ Tickets, itinerary
- ❑ Passport and necessary visas
- ❑ One or more business outfits
- ❑ Address book
- ❑ Car/hotel confirmation numbers
- ❑ Maps and directions
- ❑ Daily calendar, appointment information
- ❑ Calculator
- ❑ Notepad
- ❑ Business cards
- ❑ Medications
- ❑ Basic toiletries and makeup

❑ Reading glasses/contact lenses

❑ Cash and credit cards

❑ Small bills for tipping

Electronics:

❑ Portable phone

❑ Notebook or palm-sized computer

❑ Power adapters and cables

❑ Floppy disk drive, zip disks, CD-ROM

❑ Drive and blank disks

❑ Modem and connector cable

❑ Phone cord with connectors

❑ AC extension cord or power strip

❑ Electrical and phone adapters

❑ Pocket dictator and tapes

Presentation tools:

❑ Overhead transparencies or slides

❑ Laser pointer

❑ Handouts (or master copy)

❑ Company brochures

❑ Product samples

Office supplies:

❑ Notepaper or letterhead, envelopes

❑ Blank overnight courier forms

❑ Return address labels

❑ Mini-stapler and staples

❑ File folders, sticky notes

Miscellaneous:

❑ Money belt or pouch

❑ Portable alarm clock

❑ Neck/back pillow

❑ Earplugs and eye mask

❑ Luggage tags

Travel has become the largest international industry. Large numbers of retailers offer items geared toward the needs of travelers. Not all travel gadgets are worth your attention; however, you should consider any product that you feel will help you manage your travel hassles.

PREPARATION GOES A LONG WAY

The more you travel, the more important preparation becomes. Make lists of all the travel resources—airlines, hotels, car rental agencies— you frequently use. Categorize these services and include their contact numbers and any important details about their service.

TIP

Always keep a copy of this list with you when you travel. That way, if something happens or your plans change, you have the numbers to contact.

For safety purposes, it helps to carry one copy of everything on your person and another copy in your luggage. One traveler uses business-card-size information cards that include his name, address, insurance numbers, and contact numbers for credit card companies and banks. He then keeps several of these cards stashed away throughout his luggage and on his person, thereby guaranteeing that this information will be at hand whenever necessary.

PACKING ONLY WHAT YOU NEED—AND NO MORE

As a general rule, most travelers overpack. *Overpacking* is unnecessary and causes extra hassle.

PLAIN ENGLISH

Overpacking   Taking more items than is necessary while traveling. This extra baggage generally overburdens travelers, taking up their time and energy.

At most destinations in the developed world, one can purchase nearly anything. As for those extremely necessary and hard-to-find items (prescription drugs, contact lenses, your favorite kind of herbal tea), you won't forget them if they're included on your detailed packing list.

TIP

If you tend to overpack, lay out everything you think you need and then cut this by half.

Consider keeping a bag already packed with your essentials. How much time would you save by keeping your travel toiletries prepacked in your luggage? Organize your arsenal of travel essentials (your headphones, that little pillow, those great earplugs), and don't bother unpacking them each time you return home.

TIP

Learning to minimize your packing makes traveling less of a hassle.

Your Wardrobe

Particularly for business travel, it's necessary to keep your wardrobe looking coordinated and sharp. Create a basic travel wardrobe filled with some essentials that you can coordinate with many items. Invest in a basic suit and several coordinating shirts and accessories. Also consider reserving several pieces of clothing just for travel. By creating a designated travel wardrobe, you eliminate the hassle of having to make endless choices when you pack.

When packing, the primary objectives are to keep items organized and wrinkle-free. Putting different items in plastic bags—one for socks, one for underwear, and so on—can keep your wardrobe organized. Also keep shoes wrapped so they won't dirty other clothing.

TIP

> When packing clothing in a suitcase, rolling items will minimize the space necessary for each item and also reduce the amount of wrinkling and creasing. For nicer garments, especially dresses and suits, hanging bags greatly reduce wrinkling.

Scout Your Destination and Check the Weather

Even if you weren't in the Scouts, "Be prepared" is the lesson to be learned here. One of the best ways to reduce stress when traveling is to be prepared and know what to expect at your destination(s). Travel guides are a great resource for any traveler, business or recreational.

Besides providing information on restaurants, hotels, and sightseeing, travel books usually explore history and culture, as well as provide information on public transport and prices for everyday items. Guidebooks also include information on language, especially regional slang.

TIP

> Knowing ahead of time what to expect when you are traveling in a new city or country will help you stay calm and in control.

When planning a trip, try to be aware of any travel-related news regarding your destination. Also pay attention to news that might be affecting the city and its business community. Needless to say, checking the weather is a must.

TIP

> The Web is a great tool for travel preparation. At www. weather.com, among many other sites, you can get up-to-the-minute weather reports. Also use any popular search engine to find Web sites about the cities and areas where you will be traveling.

MAINTAIN A ROUTINE

Perhaps the most stressful element of travel is the strain it puts on your body. Crossing time zones, eating airplane food, sleeping in unfamiliar beds, and maneuvering in unfamiliar places all disrupt your normal routine. The most effective way to reduce travel stress is to be aware of the routines that you *can* maintain and to make every effort to do so.

Many people exercise to manage stress in their daily lives, and there is no reason they shouldn't continue to do so while traveling.

CAUTION

> The stress of travel, both physical and emotional, means that exercise is probably all the more necessary during travel if you are accustomed to a daily workout.

Get Thee to the Fitness Center

In response to the complaints of overstressed travelers, many hotels and airports now have fitness centers. Most of these centers have weight machines and cardiovascular machines.

Outdoor exercise, such as walking or jogging, is a great way to enjoy a new city. If schedule or circumstance won't allow for a full workout, a routine of floor exercises and stretches can significantly reduce tension and muscle tightness.

Personal Rituals

Maintaining small routines and rituals also helps you adjust to a new place. Do you usually listen to music while you get ready in the morning? If so, you might want to consider purchasing a small travel radio or set of headphones in case your accommodations don't provide such.

Do you read a little before you go to bed? Then don't forget that book you've been working on.

 TIP

> Keeping such essentials prepacked or included on a detailed packing list ensures that traveling won't disrupt your small routines.

Fuel for the Road

Perhaps the biggest challenge of all while traveling is maintaining a healthy diet. This becomes even more difficult if you are sensitive to certain foods or maintain a vegetarian or otherwise specific diet. When eating out, look for restaurants with large menus offering a variety of options. These allow you the most room to tailor your meal to suit your needs.

CAUTION

Travel can pose a serious threat to your digestive tract. Not only does your body suffer stress from the changes in dietary habits, but the stress that often accompanies travel can also affect the way you digest food.

To build up a good resistance before traveling, eat yogurt for several days before a long trip. The good bacteria in active yogurt cultures help your digestive system do its job well. Think of it as getting a tune-up before a long car trip.

FAST FOOD, CRASS MOOD

Beware of fast food. While it may be convenient, fast food contains gluttonous amounts of fat and unhealthy carbohydrates. Your body doesn't appreciate this food on a normal day, much less when you're enduring hours in an uncomfortable car or airline seat.

TIP

For emergency travel rations, carry packets of soup mix or dried fruits and nuts. Focus on foods that pack a lot of energy, without heavy grease or carbohydrates.

If you must resort to fast food (and there's no logical reason why you should), avoid the condiments (worse than the food), the highly sugared drinks (water is still free), and the calorie-laced deserts (the last thing you need while in motion).

THE EVILS OF AIRLINE "FOOD"

Airplane food is an evil deserving of its own circle in Dante's Inferno. No matter what the flight time, an airline usually schedules at least one meal or snack. Unless you are genuinely hungry, graciously decline the food. Also avoid alcohol when flying.

CAUTION

Although it can be relaxing at first, alcohol will later dehydrate your system.

To compensate for the dry air, try drinking water or juices, avoiding soft drinks, which will dehydrate your system. I suggest bringing a bottle of water with you.

TIP

Avoiding unnecessary food relieves your body from having to work overtime on digestion.

Travel breeds bad food habits. Succumbing to bad food and unhealthy mealtimes puts undue stress on your body in the long run. By watching your diet while you travel, not only will you help your digestive system, but you also help maintain the routine of your daily life, making travel less stressful on your body.

CAUTION

Be aware of your body and its needs. Travel-related over-exertion or stress on your body can cause illness. Often people return from a vacation or business trip and get sick. Days of bad sleep and unhealthy food eventually catch up with us—hence the frequency of the posttravel bug.

SLEEPLESS IN SEATTLE?

Like dietary habits, sleep is easily disrupted by travel, partly because of the stress placed on your body. Also like food habits, disrupting your sleep pattern can significantly add to the stress you experience while on the road.

Some people are lucky enough to be habitually deep sleepers. Nothing can stop them from getting a good night's sleep. Unfortunately, most of us need our own bed, our room, and our comfy pajamas to get a good night's rest. We're the ones who have trouble sleeping while we travel.

If you have trouble sleeping, pack some of your sleeping accessories. Bring your favorite pajamas and go through all the normal motions of going to bed. If you are accustomed to sleeping with earplugs or an eye mask, don't forget to bring them when you travel.

TIP

Why worry about making yourself adjust to a new environment when you can adjust the environment to your needs?

When you find yourself under a lot of stress and unable to sleep, consider relaxation techniques. Take a few moments to practice deep breathing. Do some exercises or stretches to work out the tension of the day. Or try taking a bath or indulging in some hot herbal tea.

INTERNATIONAL TRAVEL

Besides the obvious difficulties of long flights and jet lag, international travel poses the problems of navigating through a radically different everyday world. Being prepared is even more crucial to handling your stress in international travel.

The most stressful priority of international travel is keeping track of all your important documents and information. The earlier tips on getting organized are particularly helpful if you travel abroad.

Guidebooks address problems such as getting or changing money and what to expect when going through customs or immigration upon entry. Be sure to bring along any books or other information that might help you while traveling, or simply copy the necessary pages and leave the rest of the book behind.

TIP

International travel requires attention to language and cultural differences. This is when reading guidebooks can help you prepare. Most guides help you address what amenities you can expect to find in another country and what extras you might want to bring along.

TIP

Contact Kemal Cagri at Briggs Passport & Visa Expeditors when you need able assistance with paperwork and documents often required by foreign governments. Call 202-347-2240 or visit www.abriggs.com.

THE 30-SECOND RECAP

- Simple steps to organize your plans and your packing can significantly reduce your travel stress.

- Maintaining daily routines, such as diet, exercise, and sleep habits, also decreases the effects of travel stress.

- Days of bad sleep and unhealthy food eventually catch up with us—hence the frequency of the posttravel bug.

- By being aware of your body and attitude, you can maintain balanced habits and a positive frame of mind.

LESSON 10
The Time/Money/ Stress Connection

In this lesson, you learn the relationship between debt and the stress of having to work longer to pay for it, and you learn ways to keep your expenditures to a minimum.

THE MORE YOU SPEND, THE MORE YOU MUST EARN

Suppose you woke up one morning and found yourself in a society in which the typical person continually overspends. Suppose that the average person were in debt by several thousand dollars, as reflected by national credit card statistics. The people, furthermore, literally count on their next paycheck to meet monthly expenses (stressful!) and pay down credit card debt. In spending more than they earn, the people in this society work longer hours so as not to fall further behind. Hence, they have less discretionary time.

If you found yourself in such a place, where do you think you would be? If you guessed the United States, you are correct. Personal savings in the last few years have continued to dip while personal debt continues to rise. The typical person in a debt situation, in terms of liquid assets, has greater debt than savings. This may seem astounding to you, or you may understand it completely if you fall into this category.

CAUTION

When you continually spend more than you take in, you set yourself up for a life—at least in the short run—of working more and enjoying it less. And you may end up squeezing out moments of leisure time because of the obligation that you have incurred.

TIP

> In *The Millionaire Next Door,* authors Dr. Thomas Stanley
> and William Danko reveal how the typical millionaire in
> America today long ago developed a habit of living below
> his or her means. Most millionaires found a way to spend
> less than they earned week after week, month after
> month, year after year. They invested the savings and
> benefited from the compound interest that accrued.

Living within your means is one of the best techniques you can employ
for effective stress management, although it is curious that this observation is rarely cited.

Optimism Is Fine, up to a Point

U.S. Social Security Administration figures indicate that 80 percent of
Americans who retire have less than $10,000 a year to support themselves. What is worse, 50 percent have less than $5,000 per year to support themselves. The typical person between the ages of 45 and 54 has
only $2,300 in assets, and by retirement, those assets have grown to only
$19,500. "Not so bad: People will be covered by pension plans," you say?

CAUTION

> Less than half of all Americans are able to participate in
> any kind of company pension plan. Among those who can
> participate, average annual payments are less than $5,000,
> and this sum has been decreasing for many years.

Concurrently, optimism among baby boomers regarding their retirement
years is substantial, if not unwarranted. In a Gallup Poll of successful
baby boomers from Rocky Mountain states, 43 percent said that they
are not contributing to any kind of retirement plan. Twenty-five percent
said that they have not done any financial planning. At the same time,
92 percent of respondents felt that Social Security would not provide the
level of financial support they will need for retirement.

CAUTION

> The combination of insufficient savings and insufficient support in later years can only spell one thing: great masses of people working well past what would normally be considered retirement.

TAKE A WALK WITHOUT YOUR WALLET

When was the last time you went for a walk without bringing any cash, checks, or credit cards with you? All around us, household goods, professional goods, electronic gadgets, leisure items, gourmet foods, and sleek transportation vehicles abound. Too easily, we are caught up in consumerism, in what is proving to be a highly materialistic society.

One way to get in some good exercise without spending is to leave home some evening without your wallet. Walk around your neighborhood, or if you are in the vicinity of a shopping center, walk to it. As I pointed out in my book *The Joy of Simple Living,* it's a revealing test of character to walk past a row of stores without stopping in or buying something.

TIP

> Taking a walk without your wallet enables you to discover the simple pleasure of walking!

Taking a walk without your wallet diminishes impulse buys. Often, when contemplating whether to buy that item you saw on your stroll, the notion subsides and you conclude that you can do without it. If you happen to see something that makes good sense to acquire, you always have the option of returning at another time.

What if you encounter something on a walk that will save you time or hassle? So much of what is offered today is couched in terms of being a time-saver. Consult with the most successful people in your profession. Have they retained such devices? How do they use them? Whether or not such assessment is available, use a simple rule of thumb: If you value your time at $20 dollars an hour, and in a year you can save at least 50 hours, that accounts for the $1,000 purchase. If you can save more than an hour and the device will last longer than a year, the answer is abundantly clear.

TIP

> If a device will save you an hour or two a week for at least a year, you make $40,000 or more, and the device costs $1,000 or less, buy it.

MAKING FRUGALITY PAY OFF

Consider the situation in which you are thinking of buying a new car. The old one still runs well but is starting to look a bit worn. If you use your car extensively as part of a job, and clients need to perceive you as highly successful in order to do a lot of business with you, this may be a no-brainer issue: Go buy a new car.

Short of being a salesperson or in a situation in which your car is a fundamental part of your interaction with clients or customers, there is a host of issues to consider. For most people, $1,500 to $2,000 for auto-body repairs and a paint job would be more than sufficient to restore that new-car look to their vehicles. The payoff for such a maneuver is manyfold:

- The job can be done in as little as three or four days, so whatever disruption ensues, it is less than if you purchased a new car, which would either be delivered from the factory or require all kinds of dealer "prep" before you could actually drive it.

- Because of technological improvements in automobile repainting, you can easily choose among hundreds of high-quality, highly durable colors.

- Because you are retaining the same car, your annual vehicle taxes and insurance premiums do not go up.

- If you already own your car, you have no new car payments.

If you are still making payments on your car, chances are that the monthly outlay is less than a new car payment.

TIP

When you clean the interior of your car thoroughly and give it a new paint job, the combined feeling you experience closely rivals that of actually buying a new car.

This is just one example of how recycling, refurbishing, and upgrading what you already own enables you to reduce stress, save money, and ultimately continue to live within your means. Hence, you do not fall prey to the syndrome of working harder and longer to cover the debts you have incurred.

INVESTING FOR THE LONG TERM

Suppose you have two children, ages three and seven, and you intend for them to go to college. What a wonderful situation. You have a clear indication that roughly 11 years and 15 years from now, you'll need a certain sum per year for 4 years so that your child can attend a private or public university.

TIP

If you begin saving for such an eventuality now, in 11 years, you will be able to live a relatively normal life and work a relatively normal day while your children go to college.

Contrast this with what happens in far too many families: Too little is put away, even though the date the children will enter college is easily computed. Then with a few years to go, parents work harder and longer. Because they are working longer, they miss the time they could have spent with their children at ages 16, 17, and 18.

Unfortunately, by the time one of the children is ready to enter college, there still isn't enough money for the remaining college years, so the parents keep working while the child is in college. The child needs to get a job as well, which intensifies time pressure when it comes to studying. Ultimately, both parents and child experience time pressure for several years, because the parents didn't develop the discipline of saving regularly 15 years ago.

"Wait!" you say, this is a 10-minute guide on stress management. Why do I want to read about establishing a long-term savings plan? Because whether it is living within your means; saving for your child's future education; or saving for that special vacation, new home, or retirement, unless you start now, you will find yourself experiencing increasing pressure as you proceed in your career—particularly during those years you would prefer not to be working so hard.

CAUTION

Look around your office. Do you see people in their fifties and sixties who, by now, could have been well-off but still appear to be scrambling? Chances are they have not sufficiently developed the habit of investing for the future.

ASSESSING YOURSELF

If it is clear that you are heading down the same path, here are some ideas to ensure that you put aside some of your earnings today for the things that you want to do tomorrow:

- Practice the time-honored principle of paying yourself first. Every time you are paid, allocate a small amount—be it 5, 10, or 15 percent—from your paycheck and invest it immediately. There are many safe ways of investing, and any financial planner can advise you accordingly:

    Savings accounts

    Stock funds

Mutual funds

IRAs

SEPs

Keogh plans

401ks

TIP

> If it helps, have your employer automatically withdraw a portion of your paycheck so that the investment becomes automatic and you don't have to think about it.

- Continue to pay off loans after you have retired them, except now, pay yourself. For example, if you are about to pay off your car loan, the month after the loan is completely paid, redirect the usual amount paid on the car loan into your savings. Each month, continue to put the same amount into savings.

TIP

> After paying off a debt, redirecting the payment to savings shouldn't be a burden, because you are already accustomed to not having that sum of money. You are not doing anything differently, except that you now contribute to a more prosperous future.

- Do the same with pay raises. If you get a pay increase, instead of going out and immediately spending your money, invest the extra amount in some type of savings account. Again, since you are already getting by on the previous amount you were earning, it is well within your capability to invest the amount of your increase in a regular savings plan.

CAUTION

Don't fall prey to the trap of already "spending the money" in your head before you get to a new level of pay. This will only ensure that there is never enough, and well into your fifties and sixties, you will face recurrent income pressures because your debts exceed your earnings.

- Get in control of your credit cards. If, when you sum up all the debt on all your credit cards, you find that it exceeds 15 percent of your monthly take-home income, you need to limit your spending right now. Pay down your credit card balances to zero if you can, or however far down you can go.

TIP

The goal in any given month is to have credit card balances that do not exceed 10 percent of your monthly take-home income. Also, you should try to pay the whole amount so that you incur no finance charges, which tend to be exorbitant.

FOREWARNED CAN LEAD TO FOREARMED

Remember that in terms of liquid assets, the typical income-earner today has greater debt than savings. In the short term, being in a cash-deficit position can be frustrating and routinely yield feelings of pressure. In the long term, it can diminish the quality of your life.

Develop the habit now of investing a portion of your earnings every month. You can do this through automatic withdrawals from your paycheck, "paying yourself" after completing loans, investing the difference each month after you receive a pay raise, or any other method that works for you.

THE 30-SECOND RECAP

- The link between time, money, and stress is inextricable.

- When you continually spend more than you take in, you set yourself up for working more and enjoying it less.

- If you live within your means and invest wisely, financial security may be within reach.

LESSON 11

Visualization and Guided Imagery

In this lesson, you learn how to use visualization and guided imagery to help reduce stress and provide a buffer between action and reaction.

WHAT IS VISUALIZATION?

Close your eyes and imagine you're in a quiet room. No one is near, the phone is unplugged. Take a deep breath and enjoy the view in your head. Even imagine that you've already read through this book and you're a master at stress reduction. Now open your eyes. You've just practiced the basics of visualization. Don't you feel better already?

PLAIN ENGLISH

> **Visualization**   The practice of forming a mental image to foster a sense of calm and more readily focus on tasks.

TIP

> Visualization is one of the easiest, most common methods people use to reduce stress. Chances are, most people don't realize that they're doing anything special. They're simply taking a mental break and trying to clear their head before they move on to acknowledge or tackle whatever the latest stressor happens to be.

YOU'VE ALREADY BEEN PRACTICING

How many times have you been bombarded with that one last thing that forced you to close your eyes for a second, take a breath, and say to yourself, "Okay, how do I deal with this?" When you close those eyes for a little while longer and picture something specific, for example, a clean desk or a conference room full of friendly people, you're using visualization as a stress reducer.

On the home front, you might be concerned with the rising number of bills you have to pay, a noisy environment, quarrels with people in your household, and so on. In every instance, you have the opportunity to envision a more pleasant scenario.

AKIN TO MEDITATION

Visualization is similar to meditation (see Lesson 13, "Meditation"). If you can imagine yourself in a positive situation, you increase the odds of that situation actually happening. *The American Journal of Nursing* reports that visualization is both a way to create a link between the body, mind, and spirit and is frequently a valuable tool for reducing pain and anxiety in patients of all ages. In fact, using visualization techniques has been shown to improve sleep, concentration, and creativity.

Stressors cause the nervous system to respond in a way that helps the body adapt to stress. Just as a nervous moment gets your adrenaline flowing, stressors cause your body to increase its heart rate, blood pressure, and breathing, so that extra blood is transported to your lungs and muscles.

PLAIN ENGLISH

Adrenaline   A hormone secreted by the adrenal glands that acts as a powerful stimulant in times of stress.

As you've already learned, increasing the degree and frequency of these activities can cause chronic headaches, backaches, stomach aches, insomnia, muscle tension, and even irritability. Visualization techniques can help people learn to modify how stressors affect them, and in turn how their body reacts.

IF YOU THINK IT, IT CAN HAPPEN

Remember the line from the movie *Field of Dreams,* "If you build it, he will come?" They were talking about building a baseball field. Once the field was built, key players and fans would arrive. The same notion holds in reducing stress: If you imagine a calm situation, you can help to create one.

Public figures, professionals at what they do, routinely use visualization techniques to prepare themselves for big events:

- Concert pianists might close their eyes before a big performance and envision the keystrokes across the ivory keyboard.

- Golfers, before they tee off on any hole, take a few practice strokes to help visualize where the ball will go and what they need to do to get it there.

- Actors envision their scenes and directions before they perform them.

- Public speakers overcome nerves by picturing the auditorium and the audience, and visualizing themselves giving their speech. They click their imaginary slide show and run through their whole presentation, as a flawless show, before it ever happens.

- A baseball pitcher, trying to save the game in the bottom of the ninth with the bases loaded, might close his eyes and see his next pitch sailing into that perfect strike zone across the plate where the batter will miss it.

As you can see from these examples, visualization can help you sail more easily through events that have not yet happened.

IF IT'S GOOD ENOUGH FOR MCGWIRE ...

More and more of the games of baseball pitcher Mark McGwire were televised nationally as he approached the 60 home run mark, the record once held by Babe Ruth, and the 61 home run mark, the record once held by Roger Maris. If you watched Mark McGwire at the plate during any part of his home run record-breaking season or saw any of the film highlights, undoubtedly you saw Mark McGwire practice visualization in the on-deck circle before he came up to bat.

Each time he approached the on-deck circle, you could see him close his eyes, and with a slight nodding of his head, go through the motions of visualizing favorable outcomes.

In his mind (most likely) he saw the pitcher wind up and deliver the ball. He saw himself uncoil the bat and swing it around lightning fast. He saw the bat strike the ball right on the button. He saw the ball take off at a ferocious speed, much faster than the pitcher had thrown it, and at a high trajectory.

Then he saw the ball clear the home run fence, be it 380 feet, 410 feet, or 425 feet. He saw the ball land somewhere deep in the stands and a happy fan catch it. He saw himself trotting around the bases, waving to the crowd. He saw himself stepping on home plate, high-fiving the other runners.

He saw himself walk back to the dugout, with 50,000 fans screaming. He saw his teammates rise to greet him. He saw his son jump for joy. Perhaps he even saw the box score the next day listing yet another home run.

That season, at the unheard-of pace of one home run in fewer than every eight at-bats, he stepped up to the plate and made it happen 70 times officially.

McGwire had been visualizing his time at bat long before he broke the record. During that season, and since then, millions of people have been able to see this visualization realized.

Visual Shorthand

A skater who performs a four-minute freestyle routine may visualize the entire routine, second for second, for the entire four minutes. However, a marathon runner does not envision every step of the way along the 26-plus mile route. It's not practical, even if it were possible.

These runners focus on the high points, such as getting the proper rest, eating the right foods, feeling good to start the race, starting with a flourish, pacing themselves, drawing upon energy reserves, staying competitive, closing with a strong finish, maintaining composure, and so on.

TIP

When marathon runners feel good about the impending event through visualization and then do it repeatedly, they are bound to run a better race.

Handling the Contingencies

Veterans know the value of using visualization for all aspects of their performances. The veteran speaker doesn't simply imagine a perfect presentation every time. He allows for contingencies. He imagines, for example, how he'll handle the situation if the projector breaks down. The situation is much less stressful if one of these contingencies does happen, and the performer looks poised and professional if he's already played through it in his head. And so can you!

Practice Now and Often

The great thing about visualization is that it is available to you at will. In fact, you can take a stress-alleviating break right now. Close your eyes and picture pleasant scenery. This will help you clear your head and start fresh when you open your eyes.

Is your desk at work so piled with papers and projects that you can't find a place to put your latest assignment? Close your eyes and picture a clean desk, the work done, and a stress-free you. Then open your eyes and work toward that goal.

Is the phone ringing, the television a little too loud, someone knocking at the door, and kids yelling at each other? Close your eyes and picture yourself relaxing, however you might do it, oblivious to all the insanity. Open your eyes, and you'll be better able to deal with it all.

NEWTON'S LAW

One of Sir Isaac Newton's laws of thermodynamics states that "For every action, there is an equal and opposite reaction." There is an office poster that says "A lack of planning on your part does not constitute an emergency on my part!" Put some stock in this!

CAUTION

When someone rushes up to you with his world falling apart, jumping right into his mindframe won't solve any problems. Instead of one stressed and possibly irrational person, there will be two.

You can't find a clear solution without a clear head, so be the equal and opposite reaction. Someone is stressed, overwhelmed, and crying for help? For every bit he is stressed, you be calm. Take a breath, visualize a calmer person in front of you, and you will help create one! Visualize yourself with the perfect solution, and it may come true!

GUIDED IMAGERY

Visualization requires you to close your eyes and imagine a calmer situation, whereas guided imagery uses the power of positive thinking to summon thoughts and visions related to attaining specific goals.

PLAIN ENGLISH

Guided imagery An intensified use of visualization techniques to achieve a long-range goal.

In this sense, guided imagery is a mental process. It is being used with growing frequency in medicine as a means to reduce patient stress and—as you learned earlier—to help control physiological functions.

A person undergoing physical therapy to relearn how to walk might be told repeatedly to picture her left foot moving in front of her right. Eyes closed, the patient is able to envision what she wants to achieve. Slowly but surely, her mind absorbs the message and does what it can to initiate the response. This might not quite be walking. It might not even be moving the foot forward. But even moving the foot might be significant progress toward the goal of learning to walk again.

TIP

Scientists still can't explain quite why, but very often, willing something to happen is the first step toward it happening. Many doctors believe that you can almost "trick" your brain—that the more you envision something, the more real it seems to the brain. In turn, the brain sends the body more information that can work toward meeting the goal.

IT GETS PRETTY REAL

Imagine yourself scooping your favorite flavor of ice cream. The scoop is warm, and the ice cream is so cold that as you scoop it, steam comes out of the carton. You put your first scoop into a warm bowl and the scoop slides around a little. It's starting to melt, and you can almost taste it. You lick your finger where some ice cream fell. Maybe you go for a second scoop. Maybe you take out some hot fudge and pour the steaming fudge over the top.

Are you salivating yet?

You just used guided imagery to imagine a process, and your body is responding to the picture you have painted. When your mind is relaxed, it is more open to suggestion—just like when you are relaxed, you are more agreeable to new situations.

GET STARTED NOW!

Guided imagery is a popular tool for reducing stress in all sorts of situations. People practice guided imagery with coaches, counselors, confidants, physical therapists, doctors, and nurses.

Because not everyone is comfortable with expressing his or her inner-most stresses and concerns to others, many audiotapes and videotapes are available that provide nature sounds. Sounds of the rainforest, waves hitting a beach, or peaceful music encourage listeners to relax and concentrate on their senses. Listeners get involved with what they are hearing, seeing, feeling, and then are able to calmly address the stressors that have been wearing them down.

 TIP

Numerous audiotapes and videotapes are available both online and in health food stores to guide you through your imagery.

BE CAREFUL WHAT YOU WISH FOR

If there is a downside to visualization and guided imagery, it's to be careful what you wish for—you might get it. When you practice visu-alization techniques or guided imagery, conclude your visions with a positive affirmation.

 CAUTION

Picturing yourself 20 pounds thinner and imagining that you lost the weight because of a terrible illness defeats the idea of stress reduction.

Before you open your eyes, always remind yourself that you want to attain the best possible situation in the best possible way. If you head off trouble at the pass, that is one more way to reduce stress.

No Miracle Cures Here

Visualization and guided imagery are not miracle cures for your stress. While you may achieve some immediate noticeable results, as with much of what you encounter in life, there is a residual effect when putting these techniques into practice.

 TIP

The more you believe in and practice visualization and guided imagery, the greater the potential for them to take effect.

The 30-Second Recap

- Visualization is a powerful and easy tool for reducing stress— all you do is close your eyes and use your imagination!

- Visualization is one of the easiest, most common methods people use to reduce stress.

- Guided imagery—using visualization techniques with a guide—is effective therapy for dealing with life changes, working toward goals, and especially reducing overall stress.

- You can use guided imagery alone by using cassette tapes with prerecorded guided imagery programs.

LESSON 12
Breathing

In this lesson, you learn breathing techniques to help diffuse stressful situations, find a moment of calm, and tackle the stressor at hand.

FROM THE GET-GO!

Besides being the first thing we ever did in this world, breathing is a great stress reducer. Most of the time, we are completely unaware of our breathing, letting our bodies work on their own. Breathing is secondary. We don't have to command our bodies to breathe any more than we have to command our hearts to beat. The difference is, we can command our body to breathe.

Have you ever had to give a big presentation, deliver bad news, or go out in front of an audience and perform? If you have, you probably have had that "moment of truth"—that time before you step into the spotlight when you take a deep breath and whisper to yourself, "Here goes." The "here goes" part might not be therapeutic, but the deep breath certainly is.

Your body needs oxygen to perform its natural functions, for you to think, solve problems, and even to relax. When you're stressed, you breathe quickly. You might take smaller, faster breaths. Your breaths are shallower. You still take in all the oxygen you need, but in the process, you cause your body to expend more energy than it would normally.

Consider your car. It makes much more sense to fill your gas tank completely at the gas station near your house than it does to put $5 worth of gas in your car at a station five miles away and then repeat the process at other far-flung stations. Your car will run either way, but the first way is easier, and more cost- and fuel-efficient.

Breathing works the same way. If you can calm your body in an otherwise stressful situation and take slow, deep breaths, you are being more efficient with the energy your body has and how it is able to spend that energy.

TIP

In a stressful situation, it's far better to spend your energy on thinking about solving the problem and decreasing the stressor than it is to waste that energy on ineffective breathing.

NEW-AGE PSYCHOBABBLE?

Woodwind and brass musicians aspire to the perpetual breathing technique made famous by the trumpeter Louis Armstrong. He played his trumpet without ever breaking to take a breath. Instead, he was breathing continuously, inhaling through his nose and exhaling through his mouth as he played the trumpet. Today, saxophonist Kenny G. uses this method to sustain notes for astounding lengths of time. Even singers concentrate on their breathing to make their breaths less noticeable as they sing their tunes.

Athletes of all levels and abilities are always working to regulate their breathing. Runners try to establish rhythms to increase their stamina and reduce their feelings of "being winded." Swimmers practice breathing techniques to increase their lung capacity for diving and underwater swimming.

Lamaze coaches teach their patients to breathe slowly and carefully when they are in labor. Careful breathing not only reduces physical stress but also helps the mom-to-be concentrate on an activity rather than focus on the pain or being nervous.

TIP

Athletes, musicians, and even business presenters don't study breathing techniques simply to better their endurance or performance. They know that taking a deep, calm breath before initiating any activity is a simple way to reduce stress.

Breathing Techniques

Look at a healthy baby while it sleeps, and you will see the baby's little belly rise up and down in a calm, rhythmic pattern. This is because babies have not yet learned to breathe *incorrectly.* This diaphragmatic breathing, which uses the diaphragm and not the chest or shoulders to breathe, is one of the basic breathing techniques you can relearn to improve your breathing and reduce your stress.

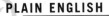

PLAIN ENGLISH

Diaphragm   A muscle at the base of your lung cavity. As it expands and contracts, the diaphragm creates a vacuum effect, using force from the middle abdomen to draw air into the lungs.

TIP

Even if you're a chest breather, if you simply take in more air each time you inhale, you'll immediately begin to feel the effects. In time, you can stabilize your blood pH level. You'll notice that you start breathing more slowly.

Stand and Deliver

While standing, a quick test to see whether you're doing diaphragmatic breathing is to place one hand on your chest and the other hand on your stomach. Now for a minute or so, breath normally (or at least what is normal for you). As you inhale, look at your two hands. Which hand moves more? If it's the hand on your stomach, you're engaged in diaphragmatic breathing. If it's the hand on your chest, you're engaged in chest or shallow breathing, which is inefficient and denies you the benefits that deeper breathing offers. If the hand on your chest moved more, chances are you not breathing with your diaphragm.

> **CAUTION**
>
> If you've been engaged in vigorous athletic activity, you may resort to using your chest and upper torso in combination with your abdomen to get oxygen into your lungs faster. This is understandable. At a normal heart rate, however, deep, diaphragmatic breathing is best.

The topic of diaphragmatic breathing has heated up in recent years. Many books, including *Breathe Better, Feel Better; Breathe to Live; Conscious Breathing; The Breathing Book*; and *Deep Breathing*, among others, offer techniques for the millions of dysfunctional breathers in today's society.

> **CAUTION**
>
> Human anatomy has been a couple of million years in the making, and chest breathing is simply not as efficient as diaphragmatic breathing.

Instruction on breathing, sometimes coupled with meditation and yoga classes, is available everywhere, from YMCAs to adult education courses, to health and fitness clubs, to international training centers. You can pay from $10 to $1,000, or you can practice the following exercise.

DIAPHRAGMATIC BREATHING

You've learned that breathing with your diaphragm uses less energy than breathing with your shoulders and chest. When you breathe naturally, your diaphragm moves in and out, giving your rib cage and your lungs more room to expand. Retraining yourself to use diaphragmatic breathing is relatively easy.

PLAIN ENGLISH

> **Diaphragmatic breathing** Focusing on expanding and contracting the diaphragm, rather than lifting the shoulders and chest cavity, in order to breathe deeply.

Follow these steps for diaphragmatic breathing:

1. Put your hand on your abdomen and inhale a deep breath. You should feel your diaphragm move down and away, expanding your rib cage. Your shoulders and chest shouldn't move.

2. Slowly exhale and feel how your diaphragm moves back to its original position.

3. Take another deep breath. Concentrate on breathing without your chest and shoulders, and try to make the breath steady and controlled.

4. Exhale, paying attention to the same factors.

5. Repeat five to six times, a few times a day, until you create a more relaxed and natural breathing pattern for yourself.

TIP

> Controlled, measured breathing can take many forms, but they all help reduce stress and help our bodies function more efficiently.

OTHER BREATHING TECHNIQUES

Many techniques for effective breathing were developed in the East—in some cases, centuries ago. This section presents a small sampling of those techniques.

CHI BREATHING

The martial arts are based largely on communicating with the spirit and finding peace (see Lesson 14, "Yoga, T'ai Chi, and Stretching"). Chi breathing, also called *dahnjeun, chi kung,* and various other names, is a technique used in the martial arts. It helps regulate and control the breathing to enhance concentration and reduce the stresses associated with the strenuous physical activity that martial arts requires.

Each discipline of martial arts offers its own breathing exercises, and many of the exercises are similar. An Internet search on "chi breathing" or a quick visit to the Martial Arts section of your library will provide you with infinite approaches to practicing the art of chi breathing, all of which are designed to increase your focus and relaxation.

NADI SHODHANA

Nadi shodhana is a yoga breathing exercise. Much like the martial arts use breathing exercises to facilitate calmness, yoga requires and helps to develop a serenity that depends on regulated and relaxed breathing.

The term *nadi shodhana* means "sweet breath" or "channel cleansing." The idea behind nadi shodhana is that you inhale through one nostril and exhale through the other, gradually creating a smooth, circular cycle.

Learning nadi shodhana is not difficult, but because you probably can't control which nostril you breathe through, you can cheat and use your fingers. Here's how to do it:

1. Place your index finger outside your left nostril. Push against your nose until your nostril is closed.

2. Take a slow, deep breath through your right nostril.

3. Now use your index finger to push your right nostril closed.

4. Slowly breathe out your left nostril.

5. Repeat these steps for up to a dozen rounds, until you feel calmer and ready to tackle the next stressor that comes your way!

CLEANSING, CLARIFYING, AND ENERGIZING

Dr. Ed Newman, based in California, has developed and synthesized some innovative techniques for effective breathing that help to reduce stress and anxiety. (Visit www.learningskills.com.) He describes three types of exercises—cleansing, clarifying, and energizing—to help you relax and breathe naturally:

- **The cleansing breath**   Sit in a comfortable position in a comfortable chair. Lie down, if you can. Close your eyes, and inhale slowly and deeply. While you are inhaling, visualize the air you are breathing. Does it have a specific color? Is it perfectly clear? Visualize the path the air takes through your body, focusing on specific body parts: your fingertips, legs, and toes.

  Then focus on exhaling all that air through some opening in your body. Be creative! Maybe you envision a valve on your knee. Open the valve and watch your air come out. Keep doing this until you can open your eyes and feel refreshed and calm.

- **The clarifying breath**   Get comfortable. Close your eyes. Take a slow, deep breath. Now pucker up those lips like a saxophone player and exhale a quick, forceful puff. Wait a few seconds, and exhale some more. Repeat this until you have emptied your lungs completely, and then inhale again to start the process over. Concentrate on the actual process, and you'll be relaxing and destressing through breathing.

- **The energizing breath**   Again, get comfortable and close your eyes, but this time, take a few deep breaths. Envision the sun, and imagine its rays reaching all the way down to touch your skin. As you take a breath, imagine inhaling the sun's rays. As you breathe in the sunlight, imagine that your body is being refreshed and rejuvenated.

  Exhale and feel the same effect of the light through your body. Repeat this activity with different colors and images until you find the one that's most energizing for you.

THAT'S IT?

That's it! Seems strange, doesn't it, that something as simple as breathing can be such an easy and efficient way to manage stress?

Yet people from all walks of life, facing all sorts of challenges, already practice this basic tenet—take a deep breath before you do anything. A simple, careful breath can act as a buffer between stress and reaction, and that buffer will help you alleviate stress from the start.

TIP

> Use breathing exercises as more than a destressor. Relearn the natural breathing techniques you were born with, and your body will operate more efficiently.

The next time someone runs up to you with a crisis, close your eyes. Take a deep breath. Imagine that you are in control. Breathe calmly, which will help you react calmly, and you *will* be calm.

THE 30-SECOND RECAP

- A deep breath can be energizing and relaxing mentally as well as physically—the slow and rhythmic intake of oxygen makes the body more efficient and reduces the physiological stress you may not even realize you'd created.

- Breathing is the most instinctive thing we do, but as we age, we forget how important it is to breathe correctly.

- Countless breathing exercises can help regulate and improve breathing. Find one that you like and practice it.

LESSON 13
Meditation

In this lesson, you learn what meditation is, different types of meditation, and how you can work the practice into your life.

WHAT IS MEDITATION?

Meditation is an ancient technique that promotes relaxation, increased awareness, mental focus, clarity, and a sense of peace. Meditation helps to focus the thought process. Many people associate the word *meditation* with certain religions and cultures, especially Buddhism and Hinduism; even Christianity has echoes of meditation phrases and rituals.

Meditation can be practiced by anyone, with or without a spiritual connection. Although it has spiritual origins and the primary use in the past was religious, meditation is now actively being explored as a way of reducing stress on the mind and body.

The typical human mind is always working, actively thinking, and filtering the sensory input that constantly bombards it. Meditation works to slow the occurrence of random thoughts and eventually stop them all together, which heightens the participant's awareness. With the recent emergence of scientific studies on how the mind can affect the body, interest in meditation has increased.

TIP

> Meditation is a matter of focus, and that focus can be on anything. The something that is contacted within you during meditation can be called *God, soul, peace, silence,* or whatever you want to call it.

A Different Discipline Altogether

Meditation is not the same as relaxation and self-hypnosis, although people mistakenly make the connection. Relaxation, in the form of activities such as watching television, does not stop the busyness of the mind the way meditation does. Watching television is *passive,* whereas meditation is an *active* process.

Although meditation begins with concentration in the same way that self-hypnosis does, it revolves around heightened awareness and consciousness of the process. Conversely, self-hypnosis leads the participant into a trance of semiconsciousness.

All forms of meditation are designed to quiet the mind. Most forms involve intense concentration on an object, a geometric drawing, a sound, or breathing. In each case, concentration is employed to stop random thoughts, which in turn calms the mind.

TIP

When the mind is calm, we can experience total peace and deep relaxation.

A Documented Discipline

The body's responses to the deep relaxation that meditation allows have been thoroughly studied and documented. Some of the demonstrated physiological changes that can occur include …

- An increase in the brain's alpha-wave activity.
- A decrease in analytic thinking.
- A decrease in metabolic rate.
- A decrease in oxygen consumption.
- A decrease in musculoskeletal tension.
- A decrease in respiration rate.
- A decrease in heart rate.

Some of the benefits of the deep relaxation that meditation induces are ...

- A reduction of generalized anxiety.

- The prevention of stress buildup.

- Increased energy.

- Increased productivity.

- Improved concentration.

- Improved memory.

- A reduction of insomnia and fatigue.

- The prevention or reduction of migraines, ulcers, and hypertension.

- Increased self-confidence and self-awareness.

TYPES OF MEDITATION

Of the many types of meditation that exist, some are strict and regulated, while some are more general. Because all types appear capable of producing the same beneficial effects, you have the opportunity to find the form that works best for you.

CHAKRA MEDITATION

Chakra meditation involves focusing your concentration on energy centers, called *chakras,* in your body. There are seven primary chakras, but the meditation only focuses on three of these energy centers.

PLAIN ENGLISH

Chakra   A concentration of energy in the human body, located along the spinal cord.

The first chakra sits at the base of the spine. Chakra meditation pulls energy from this chakra through the other chakras, ending at the last chakra in the middle of the forehead. Most practitioners start meditating at the third chakra, which is just below the naval. This releases the energy of the first three chakras and is the center of willpower and strength.

TIP

By concentrating on an energy center while meditating, you activate it and release its energy.

Next they meditate at the forth chakra, which is in the general area of the heart, in the middle of the chest. This releases the energy from the fifth chakra, too, and is the center for balance and happiness.

Finally they turn their focus to the sixth chakra, which is in the middle of the forehead. This is the center for wisdom and psychic seeing. The meditation consists of equal amounts of time spent on each chakra.

YANTRA MEDITATION

Yantra meditation involves focusing on geometric designs. The designs are called *yantras*. The theory is that the designs represent doorways to worlds of light. Focusing on a yantra can bring you happiness and clarity by connecting you to the brightness the yantra represents.

TIP

Focusing your mind on something external helps to quiet your thoughts.

You begin by focusing on the center of the yantra. The center of the yantra is also where you will bring your focus back to if you find your mind wandering. When you silence all thoughts, you can move your focus toward the edges of the yantra and eventually to the design as a whole. After a while, you will be able to close your eyes and still visualize your design.

MANTRA MEDITATION

Mantra meditation involves the repetition or chanting of a *mantra* to bring the participant to a higher level of consciousness. The sounds that you produce while chanting—out loud, in a whisper, or in your head—are a form of energy.

PLAIN ENGLISH

Mantra   A sacred word or phrase, repeated in the course of meditation as a means to focus.

Whenever your mind wanders, you bring it back to the mediation by focusing on the sacred sounds and meanings of the mantra. Your powers of concentration will be heightened if you practice chanting a mantra for the duration of your meditation.

RELAXATION MEDITATION

Relaxation meditation begins with allowing your eyes to rest in a soft, downward gaze. This has an instant relaxing effect. The benefits of this method of meditation include stress reduction and increased alertness. The act of gazing downward, with your eyelids lowered to a comfortable position, is the focus of this meditation; if you have any distracting thoughts, bring your attention back to the gaze. Your breathing will become rhythmic.

TIP

If your eyes get heavy, you can close them and focus on your breathing, on each taking in and letting out of air. Other forms of meditation use breathing in this way as the focus.

A COMMON THREAD

Each form of meditation discussed in the preceding section is simple enough to be practiced by anyone. The common thread in each of them is the intense concentration on something to free the mind from extraneous thoughts.

Here are some helpful ground rules for the meditation discussed so far:

- It is most beneficial if you meditate for at least 15 minutes twice a day.

- Try to meditate every day, and always in the same place.

- Find a special place to meditate—one that is quiet and only used for meditating.

- Always use good posture. Keep your back straight so that energy can flow up the spine.

- To avoid feeling heavy and sleepy, do not meditate right after eating.

- Take a shower or wash your hands before meditating.

- Don't seek meditation expecting to see the effects. These expectations will take away from the experience.

- Believe in the practice. There is no need to meditate if you do not believe it can work.

MINDFULNESS MEDITATION

Unlike the other forms of meditation described earlier, *mindfulness* is meditation in action. Practicing mindfulness brings meditation into all aspects of your daily life. The idea is based on the Zen Buddhist belief that whatever you focus on, you become. Knowing that, the key to mindfulness is easy to understand: If you focus on happy things, you will become happy. Positivity defines this form of meditation.

PLAIN ENGLISH

Mindfulness   The practice of focusing on the positive in all aspects of life.

TIP

To practice mindfulness, you must pay close attention to your thoughts, emotions, and reactions in all situations. When you encounter something negative, transport your mind to something positive.

TIP

Mindfulness is like any other habit—it's acquired through practice.

After you master the method, you'll notice a difference. You will not only feel happier throughout the day, but you will have more energy into the evening. By recognizing the negativity that surrounds you, you make a conscious and active effort to keep it from bringing you down. The result is a more positive outlook more of the time.

MIND YOURSELF

Walking with spirit is another form of mindfulness. Mindfulness helps to foster a state of relaxed awareness at almost any time and in almost any place. You simply focus your attention on what you're experiencing every moment.

TIP

To the degree you can, don't dwell on what you're going to do in the future, or what you've done in the past. Instead, notice what's occurring right now—in mind, body, and surroundings.

Slowly you begin to experience a nonjudgmental, greater awareness of what you're doing or what you're experiencing. You don't forsake any responsibilities or cast your fate to the wind; instead, you seize moments of your day to help you reawaken to the fullness of your life and experience on earth.

WHEN IN THE WOODS, BE IN THE WOODS

When you walk through the woods thinking about that last report you turned in, what you'll have for lunch, or that bill you have to pay, you miss the experience of the forest and all the sensory cues it has to offer. More alarming, you miss the present moment and the true experience of your life as it unfolds. You are, after all, in a forest, walking along.

 TIP

> When walking through a forest, if you notice the forest, yourself, how you feel, and what you're experiencing, you have a far greater chance of remaining relaxed, at ease, observant, and aware.

Some "walking with spirit" advocates suggest focusing on a word or phrase, as is used in the sit-down forms of mediation. Focusing on a word or phrase helps you stay centered and keeps your attention on the present. You notice your movement, and you notice your breath.

 TIP

> If you choose to utter positive affirmations, you can silence some of the negative clatter and claptrap that resonates in your head.

Here are some words and statements that spirit walkers focus on:

- Be calm.
- Be here now.

- Thank you.

- My heart is strong and healthy.

- I am at peace.

- I feel contentment.

WORKING MEDITATION INTO YOUR EVERYDAY LIFE

No single type of meditation is right for everyone, so try several types
and discover what works best for you.

CAUTION

If you fail to experience the peace of mind and relaxation
that comes with meditation, it doesn't mean that you are
practicing incorrectly or that you are not capable of concentrating. The important thing is that you meditate regularly.
Find a method that is beneficial to you and stick with it.

Some people say that the best time to meditate is in the early morning,
because things are less hectic, and that provides a more effective meditative atmosphere. It also allows you to carry the energy throughout your
day. Late evening is another good time, because you can get rid of some
of the stress you accumulate during the day. Of course, your personal
schedule is the deciding factor. Set aside the time, whenever that may be.

TIP

If you're concerned about finding the time, give up
something else. Perhaps you will spend 15 fewer minutes in front of the television, or set your alarm clock for
15 minutes earlier in the morning. You will be glad that
you did, and once you start to feel the benefits, the 15
minutes will be easier and easier to find.

With many aspects of meditation, you adjust according to what is comfortable for you. You can meditate with your eyes open or closed, for example. For some, closing the eyes is an invitation to fall asleep, but for others, it is more comfortable and less distracting.

CAUTION

When meditating with your eyes open, especially when focusing on an object of some sort, you might experience a headache. If this happens, you might be too close to the object of focus, or you might need to relax your gaze.

You can also choose whether to use music when meditating. Meditative music rather than top 40 hits can help establish a good atmosphere. It can also drown out background sounds if you have trouble finding a quiet place to meditate.

TIP

If you are having trouble getting motivated to sit and meditate, music might be for you.

How to sit is up to you as well. If you cannot feel comfortable sitting on the floor, you can meditate while kneeling, sitting in a chair, lying down, or walking. The thing to remember in any of these positions is that your back must be as straight as possible. Remember that your energy travels up your spine, and you want its journey to be as smooth as possible.

You can also choose to mediate alone or in a class. You certainly can learn meditation from books, but if you want to ensure that you're practicing correctly, you should work with a skilled teacher. A teacher can handle questions that might not be addressed in your books.

TIP

> Meditation classes are widely available, where you can learn to meditate with a group of people. This works better for some people who benefit from collective energy.

TIP

> Decide how long you will meditate. The least amount of time recommended is 15 minutes, although you can start with 5 to 10 minutes if you are a beginner. You might work up to meditations that last 20 to 30 minutes.

The frequency of your practice is up to you. Twice a day is recommended. All such decisions depend on your schedule, but the important thing is to meditate consistently if you choose to do it. Meditation is like a sport: You can only get better if you practice regularly.

THE 30-SECOND RECAP

- Meditation is an ancient practice that promotes relaxation and a sense of peace.

- If practiced correctly on a regular basis, meditation can produce deep relaxation and feelings of energy.

- There are many forms of meditation; however, any meditative practice can help you train your mind to stay focused.

- You might be concerned about finding the time for meditation, but giving up something else will be worth it once you start to feel the benefits.

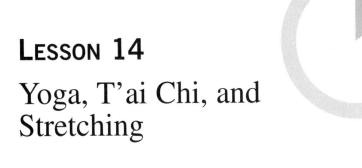

LESSON 14
Yoga, T'ai Chi, and Stretching

In this lesson, you learn about the practice of yoga, T'ai Chi, and basic stretching exercises—and how these can benefit you in your daily life.

NEW AGE EXERCISE

During the 1980s and 1990s aerobic exercise was all the rage. Jogging, biking, and aerobics classes were, and still are, popular ways to exercise and improve the body. In the twenty-first century, more people are discovering the benefits of exercise in the form of traditional meditative and martial arts practices, such as yoga and T'ai Chi.

While once upon a time such practices were viewed merely as alternatives to traditional medical and wellness practices, today traditional medical doctors are acknowledging these practices as complementary to more mainstream exercise and healthcare.

TIP

> Individuals who practice yoga, T'ai Chi, or basic stretching exercises experience the benefits of calmness, extended flexibility, increased focus, and muscle toning. The physical exertion of these activities "works off" stress and can train the body to be more balanced and focused.

YOGA

Yoga is an ancient practice involving stretching, focused breathing, improved posture, and simple meditation. The combination of these elements in the form of one exercise tends to the needs of both the mind and the body. Yoga aims to use the mind and body together, allowing them to feel the unity of their being and to rekindle energy.

PLAIN ENGLISH

Yoga   Yoga means "union," referring to the union of the mind and body.

Practicing yoga can bring a new sense of calm and balance amid the hectic environment of work and home. With regular sessions, yoga can increase relaxation, stimulate a healthier, more balanced appetite, and encourage more restful sleep. Many participants report feeling more graceful and enjoying better circulation.

Major Payoffs

Yoga participants find that each of the main components—stretching, breathing, posture, and meditation—provides long-lasting benefits for the body:

- Stretching relieves tension throughout the body and leaves you feeling lighter and more able to complete a wide range of motions.

- Regulated breathing cultivates a greater sense of awareness and helps to purify the respiratory system.

- Focusing on posture allows the body to strengthen and elongate muscles, especially those that control posture.

- Meditation improves your feelings of inner peace and contentment.

Four Basic Types of Yoga

While all yoga practices include the main elements discussed previously, the following four variations are among the most popular. Each one has been developed to achieve specific results.

- **Kundalini Yoga**   This form of yoga combines various posture techniques with meditation, chanting, and regulated breathing exercises. There's often a devotional aspect to Kundalini Yoga.

- **Hatha Yoga**   Designed to strengthen and relax the body, this practice involves a variety of elaborate exercises. Spinal twists, backbends, headstands, and similar contortions help to improve posture and promote calmness and relaxation, leaving the participant feeling "lighter." Some instructors of this practice integrate breathing exercises and meditation.

- **Iyengar Yoga**   This practice draws upon postures similar to Hatha Yoga, focusing on a more precise and refined execution of the forms. Refined muscle movements increase strength and toning. Usually chanting and meditation are not emphasized.

- **Ashtanga Yoga**   This form of yoga uses a series of postural exercises, with the goal of purifying, strengthening, and stretching the body. Typical sessions begin with a chant, followed by a long series of intense postures executed in rapid fashion with little focus on precision. This is the most physically intense of the four types of yoga.

All these types of yoga focus on postures and poses that limber up the muscles and joints of the body.

Getting Started in Yoga

You can practice yoga alone, often with the guidance of a book or video, or in a class. Many health clubs now offer yoga classes. To find a yoga instructor near you, visit the American Yoga Association Web site at www.americanyogaassociation.org.

Some Ground Rules

One of the beneficial aspects of yoga (as well as T'ai Chi and stretching exercises) is that it does not require any special equipment.

The following suggestions will make any yoga practice more comfortable and successful:

- Appropriate dress includes loose clothing and bare feet. Loose clothing allows uninhibited motion, and bare feet promote stability and relaxation.

- Practice yoga in a calm, quiet environment that allows you to focus on the exercises and meditation.

- Focus on correct breathing—inhaling through the nose while using the diaphragm (breathing from the belly). Slowing your breathing and taking the time to focus on each posture will give you more relaxation benefits.

 TIP

Working in front of a mirror allows you to watch your body's movements and improve your execution of postures and poses.

CAUTION

During your early ventures into yoga, be aware that none of your movements should cause you pain or discomfort. With increased practice of yoga, the body becomes more limber, and postures are easier to execute.

YOGA CLASSES

A basic yoga session with an instructor usually lasts for 60 to 90 minutes. Class begins with warmup breathing exercises, then moves into 25 to 50 minutes of poses involving sitting or lying down. With the next set of poses, also lasting 25 to 50 minutes, the participants move to standing postures, followed by concluding poses.

A well-planned routine should include postures and counterpostures, which work together exercising complementary muscle groups, such as quadriceps and hamstrings. You can practice similar routines independently, tailoring the movements and the length of practice to your needs.

TIP

As little as 15 minutes a day of yoga can bring lasting benefits.

STRETCHING EXERCISES

If yoga doesn't suit you, plenty of stretching exercises can give you similar benefits. Simple stretching is actually necessary for physiologic survival. When a muscle contracts, tiny fibers within the muscle glide past one another in an interlacing pattern much like interlocked fingers.

When a muscle stretches, these fibers loosen and slide back the other way. All muscles have complements—muscles that control the opposite movement. A balanced body allows its muscles freedom from overcontraction or overstretching.

CAUTION

If one set of muscles remains permanently contracted because of, say, exercising too heavily, then the other set must remain permanently overstretched to compensate for this. Neither state is healthy for the muscle.

LIFE THROWS UP CHALLENGES

The movements and positions of daily life often adversely affect the muscle groups, causing them to contract and tighten. Not only is it uncomfortable to feel stiff and tight at the end of the day, but it is unhealthy for your body's stress level.

CAUTION

Sitting in a desk chair for long periods of time and leaning over materials to read can cause tightness and cramping in muscles.

Keeping any set of muscles contracted for a long period of time engages them in the fight-or-flight mode discussed in the first few lessons. Tight muscles signal the brain to prepare for a stressful situation, and the brain in turn signals the muscles and tightens them even more. This cycle quickly increases the amount of stress put on your body, causing more discomfort and threatening your health.

FLEXIBILITY BENEFITS

Regular stretching is the fundamental, primary means to improve flexibility. It is not an exaggeration to say that increasing your flexibility dramatically changes your daily life, allowing …

- More freedom of movement.

- Wider range of motion.

- Less bodily strain from daily activities.

Have you ever noticed people who move in a particularly graceful manner? Quite likely, this is simply the result of their flexibility and range of motion. Their flexibility allows them to move with little resistance, making their movements appear easy and graceful.

BASIC STRETCHING

Stretching exercises are simple and target a particular muscle group or muscle. To achieve the most benefits from stretching, you should try to stretch regularly, preferably every day.

TIP

A safe and healthy stretching exercise involves holding a comfortable position for at least 10 seconds. The stretch should pinpoint the muscle group, allowing you to feel the muscles without experiencing pain or putting too much pressure on your joints.

While you hold a stretch, focus on taking deep breaths. This not only has a wonderful relaxing effect, but with each deep breath, the muscle expands and stretches a teensy bit more.

CAUTION

An unfortunate leftover from the high-impact aerobics era is the idea of bouncing as you stretch. Bouncing-type stretches are more harmful than helpful. They can put too much pressure on joints, causing injury. People often pull or injure muscles by accidentally bouncing too hard and forcing the muscles.

Many health and fitness magazines outline different stretches that are appropriate. You also might want to contact a fitness instructor or personal trainer and ask for stretching suggestions.

CAUTION

Regardless of your source for a stretching posture, you should discontinue any movement that causes excessive discomfort or pain.

T'AI CHI, NOT CHAI TEA

T'ai Chi (pronounced *tie-CHEE*) is a martial arts form with an emphasis on philosophy. The movements of T'ai Chi are like a formal routine, designed to balance the muscles and joints through movement, deep breathing, and manipulation of the diaphragm. The combination of graceful movements is designed to help you experience a more even temperament and a more tranquil mind.

The practice of T'ai Chi grew out of exercises used by monks to stay healthy. In its purest practice, T'ai Chi focuses on a philosophy of individuals training to devote themselves to others. One school of thought says that altruistic people have fewer stress-related problems. So, to instruct others is to achieve greater peace of mind for oneself.

Though opposing, *yin and yang* forces coexist and work in unity. Similarly, the different movements of a T'ai Chi routine are designed to flow together in a smooth unity.

PLAIN ENGLISH

Yin and yang   This symbol represents the two coexisting forces in the universe.

SIMPLICITY IN MOTION

One of the primary attractions of T'ai Chi is the relative simplicity of the practice. No special equipment is needed, except an open mind and body. Anyone can master T'ai Chi, regardless of age, gender, or even mental ability. The gentle and rhythmic movements can increase flexibility and endurance, although these characteristics are not prerequisites for the practice.

TIP

If you're an older adult, T'ai Chi may well be worth investigating, because it promotes increased flexibility, strength, and balance, while relieving pain from ailments such as arthritis.

Novices start off learning a full routine of T'ai Chi movements. Simple-form routines involve 24 movements, beginning with simple

and advancing to more complex movements. The goal is to execute
the movements slowly, carefully, and gracefully. This allows you to
focus on fostering a sense of inner peace.

TIP

> T'ai Chi practitioners recommend one session in the
> morning and one in the evening. Many people find that
> their lunch hour is a good time to fit in a short routine,
> however. This can also bring the benefits of recentering
> and renewing energy before an afternoon of work.

Go to Class

Considered a martial art, T'ai Chi is taught in many martial arts
schools in the United States. Unlike most martial arts, T'ai Chi is not
taught as a self-defense method but as a discipline to unify the body
and mind. Classes are fairly small—15 to 30 people—with plenty of
room for individuals to move freely. In many cities, it is now popular
to hold T'ai Chi classes outdoors, in open parks or gardens.

When a group is first learning T'ai Chi, the instructor focuses on
teaching an entire routine. With time, as the students learn the routine,
more emphasis is placed on the careful execution and quality of the
individual movements, focusing on specific postures, balanced shoulders, feet and hand positions, and so on.

A T'ai Chi class typically begins with everyone assuming a neutral
stance—that is, standing comfortably. The instructor might ask students to pick a focal point and to be aware of their breathing. Once
relaxed, the class is guided through a range of movements. Like any
exercise class, the instructor should demonstrate the move. Responding in unison, the class tries to emulate the grace and control of the
instructor's movements.

The instructor reminds students to pay attention to their movements,
making them flow together in a seamless, smooth motion. During the
routine, the instructor might call attention to breathing and remind students to clear their minds and focus carefully on their movements.

Under calm guidance and in a quiet environment, the rhythmic and repetitive movements begin to sooth your body and mind into a balanced, happy state. Go ahead, you can even smile.

> Different instructors may conduct their classes using different techniques. Some may include a break in the routine, while others prefer a continuous exercise. An instructor might also conduct a class focusing on specific hand or foot techniques, such as holding, punching, and pushing.

FINDING THE RIGHT FIT

No single exercise form works for every person. You might prefer the flexibility exercises of yoga to the rhythmic repetitions of T'ai Chi. If yoga and T'ai Chi represent new and different practices to you, they may seem more approachable under the guidance of an instructor.

> If you do not feel comfortable with yoga *or* T'ai Chi, perhaps stretching is more your style.

> Regardless of your fitness goal, research has shown that you need to enjoy your exercise in order to stay motivated and satisfied with the results.

In one study, Western women seemed to enjoy yoga more than men. The women felt more satisfaction in the results of their workouts. As one researcher said, "It's impossible for laboratory studies to capture the simple pleasure of doing what you enjoy, but we know it's got to be important."

THE 30-SECOND RECAP

- Yoga, stretching, and T'ai Chi are all low-impact forms of exercise that benefit the mind and body.

- Yoga practices focus on a combination of stretching, posture, meditation, and breathing.

- Basic stretching, without meditation or specific breathing patterns, also increases strength and flexibility.

- T'ai Chi focuses more specifically on rhythmic and repetitive motions to calm and focus the mind and body.

- Yoga, stretching, and T'ai Chi can be done alone or with a group. Brief routines can bring you great benefits in stress reduction and increased peace of mind.

LESSON 15
The Spas Have It

In this lesson, you learn about the growing popularity of spas and how they can help you reduce stress.

SPAS AND SUCH

In agriculture, to produce more crops, you have to cultivate the land. The same is true for the working body. Often overwhelmed by stress and too many tasks, the human body needs some "tending" to produce to its full potential both physically and mentally.

The idea of visiting a spa may seem intimidating to many people and alluring to others. As more people discover the benefits of these palaces of pampering, the range of options continues to widen to include something for almost everyone.

Down nearly every scenic highway in America, you'll find a vacation spa. Depending on where you go and what you want to pay, your experience can be anywhere from stress-reducing to sublime beyond words. The programs you encounter may range from hour-long to daylong. You'll find employees dressed in white clinician's outfits or smocks carrying clipboards, as well as digital equipment, wall charts, lotions and potions, and reading to turn your quivering mass of flesh into a serene, purring, contented body.

Luckily, spas and all their wonderful benefits are no longer reserved for high-society women and aging beauty queens. Services offered by contemporary spas cater to the needs of women *and men* of all ages and lifestyles. Isn't progress toward gender equality great? Everyone deserves the opportunity to feel good about themselves and to work away some stress.

NOT SO NEW

Many spas today offer treatments with all-natural ingredients that tone and improve the body. New Age thinking has resulted in some spas approaching body care with a holistic mindset: Improving the body can also improve the mind and spirit.

Spas seem like a natural offshoot of the leisure age. Many of the ideas and concepts behind modern spas originated in age-old traditions, however, and many are drawn from other cultures. Some of the most fascinating ruins of the ancient world were once centers of body care. The Roman baths, sizable complexes even by modern standards, were considered essential to all metropolitan centers in their day. Even the rough and tumble Britons on the northern outskirts of the empire had a huge complex built over natural springs. The city of Bath, England, takes its fame from the well-preserved ruins of a complex of Roman baths built in its center.

Bathing and personal grooming were considered essential in the highly civilized Roman Empire. All people used the public baths at least once a day. Bathing by Roman standards involved an intricate sequence of coating one's body in cleansing oils, sitting in a steam room, and taking a dip—first in warm water and then in a cooler pool. It worked for Augustus Caesar, and it can work for you, too.

ENTER A NEW SPACE

A spa creates a setting that caters to its clients' needs. Unlike your home or workplace, spas are physical spaces designed to calm and soothe the body and soul. Perhaps the most beneficial aspect of the spa experience is this removal from your daily surroundings, allowing you to let go of the stress that bogs you down.

The Web site for one spa in the Midwest reads, "… please leave your pantyhose, makeup, and heels at home. Suits, ties, and briefcases, too." The beauty of the modern spa is that in a world of high-pressure work and less-than-rewarding leisure, spas are a retreat into a relaxed space.

TIP

> Many spa services—such as aromatherapy, manicures, pedicures, and facials—certainly can be obtained elsewhere. When you go to a spa, though, you set aside time in a relaxed and conditioned environment, under professional treatment. You just can't duplicate that overall experience at home or around town.

A visit to a spa also creates a new space in your temporal landscape. Time set aside for spa treatment is specifically designed to be free of stress and strain.

It may seem challenging to take time away from your work or home environment for something that others may see as frivolous. However, this time commitment leaves you with a lasting sense of balance and renewed energy. Ultimately, the reward for making personal time for yourself at a spa is a chance to minimize stress and recharge your work and personal life.

SERVICE SUPREME

The range of services offered by spas varies greatly depending on the center. Generally spas include the basics, such as massage work and various facial treatments. Some offer more intense treatments, such as full body wraps or intensive skin peels.

Some spas focus on natural therapies that draw on traditional ingredients and treatments. One spa in Florida offers treatments such as a sea-salt body polish, mud therapy, and vitamin C and seaweed anti-aging treatments. Other spas offer modern treatments using the latest technology in products and procedures.

Some spas focus on massage and hydrotherapy techniques to improve circulation and alleviate joint and muscle pain. Most spas aim to combine the best of both worlds, offering up-to-date services that use natural ingredients, such as herbs.

TIP

> Like all personal services, getting the most out of your spa experience depends on knowing what you prefer. If you've always wanted to indulge in a volcanic mud treatment or experience the latest technique in hair removal, do your research and choose accordingly.

SHORT BREAK, ANYONE?

If you live in a city or suburban area, you can find spas in the phone book. Suppose that you want to take only a short break from your routine. You're likely to find a bevy of day spas that can cater to your needs. If not, a *day spa* or salon is probably just a commuter flight or short drive away.

PLAIN ENGLISH

> **Day Spa**   Spas that offer an abundance of services in a menu format, by appointment or to walk-in clients, allowing you to pick and choose what appeals to you (and your pocketbook and time allowance). Most urban centers now have day spas.

A day spa offers the flexibility and convenience of a short getaway. For career professionals, as well as at-home spouses, this sort of spa often provides the most manageable break. Whether you make time for one treatment, such as an hour-long facial, or an entire day of treatments, you still have the benefit of getting away for a little while.

WELCOME TO NIRVANA

At a certain spa in Virginia, you're led down a long hallway and into a private room where the sounds of the outside world are muted completely. A spa professional asks you to take whiffs of various scents to determine which one is most pleasing to you. The oil you select will be used during your massage. You are told to completely disrobe and lie on an elevated, *ergonomically* designed cot.

PLAIN ENGLISH

Ergonomics   The science that examines how devices should most smoothly blend to the human body and human activity.

The cot offers the right support under you, in all the right places. You place your head face down in a cushioned ring, which supports the perimeter of your face while leaving the broad expanse in the center of your face exposed.

RELAX, STAY A WHILE

The spa professional may ask you a few questions, such as whether you are presently in pain anywhere, whether you have been injured, or whether there is anything specific you would like to have done during this session.

Then the therapist goes to work on you. Many start at the top of the head and work all the way down to the feet. Perhaps they play New Age music or light a candle or incense. After a couple of minutes of gentle rubbing, you won't care.

Later you may be led to a whirlpool bath or a shower. You may be placed in a chair, where your spa professional will continue with a frontal massage, including your legs, arms, and face.

WORK ON THE SURREAL YOU

Your program may include a facial. Your face may be covered with some type of moisturizing cream, a mudpack, or something else designed to make you feel tingly all over. Your eyes may be covered with cucumbers.

Your seat may tilt back, at which time your hair is covered with oils and worked over gently with fingers that deftly cover every square inch of your scalp until you feel you've died and gone to heaven. Then your hair is shampooed, maybe twice over, conditioned, and then rinsed with warm, relaxing water. All the while, you forget where you're from, your name, and all the other once-important information about yourself.

Perhaps you're handed a refreshing blend of yummy carrot, papaya, or some other juice concoction designed to replenish any of the fluids you may have lost. At this point, your spa professional may describe to you what transpired during your treatment.

A potpourri of services is available to you at the spa:

facials	aromatherapy facials	manicures
pedicures	exfoliation	hydromassage baths
Swedish showers	mineral baths	hydrotherapy
herbal wraps	herbal steam showers	oil treatments
scalp massages	shampoos	haircuts
hair styling	hair coloring	body wraps
body polish	waxing	body masques
sea-algae body treatments	body scrubs	deep-tissue massages
reflexology	polarity therapy	sports massages
liver-and-whey shakes	fruit smoothies	guava juice
papaya juice	carrot juice	tea and scones

EQUAL ACCESS

A movement is afoot to get the heretofore reluctant gender into spas in larger numbers. Spa owners lament that even in the early twenty-first century, most men still don't see the value of these services. Some think it's a prissy, sissy kind of thing to do.

These days, almost all spas cater to men as well as women. Increasingly, men are realizing that looking good and feeling good go hand in hand. The Elizabeth Arden Red Door Salon and Spa, one of the first to open its doors, now caters to mens' special needs with a package called "Executive Escape." Many other spas offer similar packages that aim to relieve the stress of the working professional.

Men who have gone the spa route generally become advocates. They come seeking more vigorous massages perhaps, and leave discovering that their perpetually stiff necks don't need to stay that way.

Once men get to a spa, they are far more amenable to some of the other services that are offered in addition to massage. Reportedly, even the toughest men relent to skin cleansing, moisturizing masques, and facial scrubs.

FINDING THE PERFECT FIT

As public interest grows, the spa choices available also greatly increase. Finding a spa can be as easy as checking the phone book or searching the Web. You can contact a spa to find out about the range of services offered. Many Web pages describe the different treatments and the focus of each spa. Also, this can be a good way to find out about any packages or special spa offerings.

 TIP

> A spa should also be able to give you information about its employees. Make sure that spa technicians are certified to provide their services. Massage therapists, for example, should be certified. This ensures that their skills and knowledge have been reviewed and approved by professionals in their field.

In a world of fast-paced work and career- or domestic-related stress, spa treatment can be very beneficial to helping you maintain a healthy body and giving you more confidence. And with the variety offered today, it is possible to find something that suits your needs and makes you comfortable.

THE 30-SECOND RECAP

- Unlike home or work, spas are physical spaces designed to calm and soothe the body and soul. One of the best aspects of the spa experience is the removal from your daily surroundings.

- Spas have more to offer now than ever before. With a range of services and treatments offered on hourly, daily, or weekly schedules, spas can be a great way to treat yourself and relieve stress.

- By choosing what suits your needs, a spa experience can be fulfilling and relaxing.

LESSON 16
Profound Choices

In this lesson, you learn how and why the choice to have less stress in your life is yours for the taking.

THE POWER IS WITHIN YOU

Imagine that you had the power to reduce stress, be more balanced, and live life with greater grace and ease merely by choosing to do so. Guess what? You do! If you feel flustered, you can choose to embody grace and ease. If you're swamped by information, you can choose to have clarity.

Making profound choices is a simple but deceptively powerful way to keep stress in check while handling the challenges that life throws at you—whether it's learning new technology, surviving a merger, or being laid off.

 TIP

Choosing is not synonymous with "positive thinking" and is not some type of feel-good formula. You make choices independent of how you feel. You gain power by directly addressing what you want or how you want to feel. By constantly making positive choices, you broaden your horizons while keeping stress in check.

AUTOMATIC REDIRECTION

Robert Fritz, author of *The Path of Least Resistance,* teaches that by making choices (positive affirmations to yourself regarding what you want), you move closer each day to attaining your goals. This is not synonymous with "positive thinking." The choices Fritz suggests are made regularly, regardless of how you feel at the moment you're making them. Your goal is to keep making them.

Fritz offers these primary choices that each of us needs to make on a regular basis:

- I choose to be free.

- I choose to be true to myself.

- I choose to be healthy.

- I choose to be the predominant creative force in my life.

Making choices is a quick, silent process. You simply repeat a choice to yourself and allow it to sink in—that's it! By making important choices (such as the ones discussed in this lesson), you redirect yourself to accept that there is nothing you *must* do. Everything is based on your choice. If you choose to continue working on some task, even one assigned to you, the choice is made in the present moment rather than on a prior agenda.

The new sense of control over your life that you'll feel will yield a tremendous sense of inner harmony, as well as preserve and broaden your sense of tranquility.

For example, you may say to yourself, "I choose to …"

- Feel good about my successes.

- Capitalize on my successes.

- Maintain perspective on my successes.

- Acknowledge that career success is different from personal happiness.

- Maintain humility.

- Broaden my definition of success to include a social component.

- Be a mentor to others.

- Include others in my success.

- Acknowledge those who have made a difference in my life.

- Share the secrets of my success with others.

- Be open to new opportunities for success.

- Look forward to each workday.

- Approach my work with joy.

- Make my workplace convenient, productive, and enjoyable.

- Acknowledge my work as worthwhile.

- Celebrate the workplace.

- Engage in work that is profitable and sustaining.

- Maintain a proper balance between work and rest.

- Approach my work with a sense of discovery.

- Maintain distinctions between my self-worth and net worth or occupation.

- Celebrate Monday mornings.

- Take appropriate vacations and return to work renewed.

- Keep the tasks I face in perspective.

 TIP

> By making such choices, you reinforce how you want your life to be, and little by little, you move in that direction!

IMPROVISE AND MOVE ON

Eventually, go beyond the choices offered here and devise those that uniquely serve your purposes. Such personalization will give you the best and most lasting chance for peace of mind.

TIP

You can make choices that are not congruent with your history. You can makes choices that no one has ever made before.

An Example of Grace Under Pressure

Here's a career-related choice that I made in a potentially stressful situation. The only time I've ever been late in my 16-year speaking career occurred in November 1992. I had booked the first flight out of the Raleigh-Durham International airport on my trip to Washington, D.C. I was to speak to the U.S. Treasury Executives Institute at 9:00 A.M. I was scheduled to fly at 6:50 A.M., and the flight time was only 35 minutes. There were several other flights to D.C. leaving soon after mine on other airlines, so I felt reasonably assured that I would be at my speaking engagement on time.

Have We Got News for You!

Seconds after we rolled onto the runway, the pilot announced that there would be a delay. "No problem," I thought. "I'll still be there with plenty of time." After 10 minutes, I became concerned. Finally, another announcement came. We would have to go back to the gate because something was wrong with the plane. Now I was steamed. We were way behind schedule, and even if I could get on another plane within 10 or 15 minutes, I would arrive at Washington National Airport at 8:15 or 8:20 A.M., and that would be pushing it to arrive at the site with grace and ease before 9:00 A.M.

The airlines have a trying habit of waiting until you're in their planes, seated, and ready to roll before they announce delays. (Actually, it's not a habit, it's a strategy. If they announced such delays in the terminal, they would lose half their passengers to other flights and other airlines.)

Had I known about the potential delay, I could have quickly gotten on one of several other flights. In this case, I suppose the pilot didn't know that there was going to be a problem until he got to the runway.

TAKE TO THE SKIES

Finally we departed for D.C. and landed at about 8:40 A.M. I called the client from the airport. Then I quickly jumped into a cab and prayed that this driver could get through the D.C. morning rush hour and get me to the site somewhere close to 9:00 A.M. In the back of the cab, I had a choice to make: I could be totally stressed out over being late on so momentous an occasion, or I could make choices in light of the morning's events and be free to direct my energy more appropriately.

Here's what I chose:

- To *proactively* approach this challenge

- To maintain my composure

- To easily reassure the client

- To handle the situation like a professional

- To start my presentation with vigor

Rather than stress out, I repeated these choices over and over for the entire trip. When I finally arrived on site, I immediately was ready to proceed. The presentation turned out to be one of my best.

PLAIN ENGLISH

Proactive   The act of making choices and determining your own attitude, as opposed to being *reactive* and letting circumstances control you.

What kinds of choices will you make in the coming weeks and months?

A PARTING LETTER

Dear Stress, Complexity, and Time Pressure:

I am pleased to meet you! I realize that you'll always be present in my life, so once and for all, I'm going to learn how to keep you in check and take control. I will become more productive and energetic, yet more balanced and happier than I have been in many years. As such, I welcome you into my life, embrace you, and invite you to be yourself.

Although it's true that I've had problems with you in the past, I have now chosen to take back my power and to keep you in your place. With this simple guide, I've discovered that it's no longer necessary to give you opportunities to upset, confound, or overwhelm me. Although you'll occasionally triumph, I resolve to keep you in check. I have gathered and will continue to gather the insights and the tools I need to ensure that I maintain mastery over you.

There have been times when you seemed invincible. Those times will diminish in duration and frequency. When you exert your influence dramatically, I will be equal to the task. I'll devise brilliant counterstrategies to keep you in your place. I'll also engage in preemptive strikes to ensure that you don't gain a foothold where you're not wanted—pretty much everywhere in my life.

You've been quite a teacher, showing me where I've strayed in the past, and for that I thank you. I have made the choice to move forward, however, and as you're about to see, your effects will no longer have any lasting or significant impact.

Yours truly,

Your New Master

THE 30-SECOND RECAP

- You have the power to reduce stress, be more balanced, and live life with greater grace and ease merely by choosing to do so.

- You make choices independent of how you feel. You gain power by directly addressing what you want or how you want to feel.

- Primary choices fortify each of us, including choosing to be free, choosing to be true to yourself, choosing to be healthy, and choosing to be the predominant creative force in your life.

- You can make choices that are not congruent with your history and even choices that no one has ever made before.

APPENDIX A
Glossary

adrenaline   A hormone secreted by the adrenal glands that acts as a powerful stimulant in times of stress.

aerobic   In the presence of oxygen.

affiliate   Associating yourself with others of the same interests or goals.

alarm response   The initial recognition of a threat or demand; the first stage of the stress response.

aromatherapist   A professional using essential oils and herbs to treat clients' specific health and stress-related conditions.

aromatherapy   Use of essential oils and herbs to treat specific health and stress-related conditions.

burnout   A specific type of stress that involves diminished personal accomplishment, depersonalization, and emotional exhaustion.

cardiovascular   Pertaining to the heart and blood vessels.

carrier oils   Odorless extracts from plant life used to dilute the concentration of essential oils.

cellular intelligence   The ability of the body down to the cellular level to respond to stimuli in the immediate environment.

chakra   A concentration of energy in the human body, located along the spinal cord to the top of the head.

chronic stress   Long-term, unrelenting, potentially health- or life-threatening stress that often is unrecognized by the victim. Continuous and unremitting demands on an organism to change.

compromise   A settlement in which both sides make concessions, or a solution that is midway between two alternatives.

conflict management   Strategies for the resolution of sharp disagreements, of interests or ideas, or emotional disturbances.

diaphragm   A muscular partition between the chest and the abdominal cavities.

diaphragmatic breathing   Breathing from the partition at the base of your lung cavity. As the diaphragm expands and contracts, it creates a vacuum effect, using force from the middle abdomen to draw air into the lungs. Expanding and contracting the diaphragm, rather than lifting the shoulders and chest cavity, to breathe deeply.

environment   One's surroundings; in the context of the workaday world, one's office and surrounding offices and, in general, one's workplace.

ergonomics   The science that examines how devices should most smoothly blend to the human body and human activity.

essential oils   Liquid, concentrated extractions from flowers, fruits, trees, herbs, and resins used for therapeutic purposes. Derived exclusively from the plant; not diluted or mixed with another substance.

eustress   Beneficial stress that enables you to function more effectively, maintain concentration, strive to meet challenges, or seek thrills or excitement.

exhaustion   A state in which the body's resources have been used up, tired out, or completely emptied or drained, and the body is no longer capable of remaining alert.

fight-or-flight response   Automatic response to stimuli, real or perceived, that enables the human body to deal with a threatening situation. Mobilization of an organism's resources to deal with a threat or challenge physically or to run away from a threat or challenge.

guided imagery   The intensified use of visualization techniques to achieve a long-range goal.

job stress   The physical and emotional response to harmful working conditions, including circumstances in which the job requirements exceed the capabilities, resources, or needs of the worker.

mantra   A sacred word or phrase repeated in the course of meditation as a means to focus.

massage therapist   A professional who is trained and skilled in kneading and rubbing parts of the body to promote circulation and relaxation.

meditation   Quieting the conscious mind and allowing it to roam freely without intentional direction. Or allowing the mind to focus on a single thought or sound, intended to provide mental rest and enlightenment.

microsleep   A 10- to 15-second undiscernable sleep episode in the middle of the day.

mindfulness   The practice of focusing on the positive in all aspects of life.

motivating stress   Stress that stimulates and challenges you, as opposed to preventing you from accomplishing tasks.

neurotransmitters   Chemical messengers that trigger the brain to dispatch information that controls brain-wave activity and patterns, blood pressure, breathing, heart rate, glandular activity, hormonal production, and—you guessed it—stress levels.

overpacking   Taking more items than necessary while traveling; toting extra baggage that overburdens you and consumes more time and energy to handle.

perfectionism   The need to be in control of situations; fear of making mistakes and looking like a failure.

physiologic   Consistent with an organism's normal or expected functioning.

physiological stress   Demands on bodily systems.

physiology   The science that deals with the processes and functions of living organisms.

priorities   The things that are most important to you.

proactive   The act of making choices and determining your own attitude, as opposed to being *reactive* and letting circumstances control you.

procrastination   To put off doing a task, to delay an activity or task, or to ignore something that demands your attention.

quiet time   An interval during the day when you are not subjected to noise.

reframe   To observe in a new light or approach from a different perspective.

relaxation response   An organism's return to a state of low arousal, analogous to turning off the stress response.

respiratory system   Your lungs, bronchi, trachea, and nasal passages.

scanning   Reviewing any lists, charts, or exhibits in a book; reviewing the index, the table of contents, some of the chapter leads, and an occasional paragraph.

skimming   Reading only the first few sentences of each paragraph within an article in a magazine or on the Web, or in a chapter of a book.

sleep debt   The amount of time you add to a typical night's sleep to make up for missed sleep.

stress   The effect on an organism when under a threat or challenge or when required to change.

stress response   The physiological reaction when an organism is exposed to change; the mobilization of bodily resources and changes in bodily functions that occur when you perceive jeopardy or a threat.

stressor   An undesirable or unpleasant situation to which the body responds with fight-or-flight reactions.

stressors   Any agent that causes an organism to be under stress.

visualization   The practice of forming a mental image to foster a sense of calm and to more readily focus on tasks.

yin and yang   The two coexisting forces in the universe—the negative and the positive.

yoga   Yoga means "union," referring to the union of the mind and body.

APPENDIX B
Further Reading

Balch, James and Phyllis. *Prescription for Nutritional Healing.* Garden City Park: Avery Publishing Group, 1997.

Benson, Dr. Herbert. *The Relaxation Response.* New York: Avon, reissue, 1990.

Bhajan, Yogi, Ph.D., and Gurcharan Singh Khalsa, Ph.D. *Breathwalk: Breathing Your Way to a Revitalized Body, Mind, and Spirit.* New York: Broadway Books, 2000.

Bruce, Debra and Harris McIlwain. *The Unofficial Guide to Alternative Medicine.* New York: Macmillan General Reference, 1998.

Cathcart, Jim. *The Acorn Principle.* New York: St. Martin's Press, 1998.

Cousens, Gabriel, M.D., with Mark Mayell. *Depression Free for Life.* New York: Morrow, 2000.

Daniels, Aubrey, Ph.D. *Bringing Out the Best in People.* New York: McGraw-Hill, 1994.

Davidson, Jeff. *Breathing Space: Living & Working at a Comfortable Pace in a Sped-up Society.* New York: Mastermedia, 2000.

——. *The Complete Idiot's Guide to Managing Stress.* New York: Alpha Books, 1999.

———. *The Complete Idiot's Guide to Managing Your Time.* New York: Alpha Books, 1999.

———. *The Complete Idiot's Guide to Reaching Your Goals.* New York: Alpha Books, 1998.

———. *Joy of Simple Living.* Emmaus, PA: Rodale Books, 1999.

Devi, Nischala. *The Healing Path of Yoga.* New York: Three Rivers Press, 2000.

Domar, Alice, Ph.D., and Henry Dreher. *Self-Nurture: Learning to Care for Yourself as Effectively as You Care for Everyone Else.* New York: Viking Press, 1999.

Drucker, Peter, Ph.D. *The Effective Executive.* New York: Harper & Rowe, 1967.

Dyer, Wayne, Ph.D. *Staying on the Path.* Carson, CA: Hay House, 1995.

Farr, Mary. *The Heart of Health: Embracing Life With Your Mind and Spirit.* New York: John Wiley & Sons, 2000.

Fritz, Robert. *Path of Least Resistance.* New York: Ballantine Books, 1989.

Glenmullen, Joseph. *Prozac Backlash: Overcoming the Dangers of Prozac, Zoloft, Paxil, and Other Antidepressants with Safe, Effective Alternatives.* New York: Simon & Schuster, 2000.

Gurmukh. *The Eight Human Talents.* New York: Cliff Street Books, 2000.

Johnson, Will. *Aligned, Relaxed, Resilient: The Physical Foundations of Mindfulness.* New York: Shambhala, 2000.

Krucoff, Carol and Mitchell Krucoff, M.D. *Healing Moves: How to Cure, Relieve, and Prevent Common Ailments With Exercise.* New York: Harmony Books, 2000.

Maharishi Mahesh Yogi. *Transcendental Meditation: Serenity Without Drugs.* New York: Signet, 1963.

Markham, Ursula. *The Elements of Visualization.* Rockport, MA: Element Books, 1989.

Miller, Lyle, Ph.D., and Alma Dell Smith, Ph.D. *The Stress Solution.* Washington, D.C.: American Psychological Association, 1997.

Mitchell, Stewart. *The Complete Illustrated Guide to Massage.* New York: Barnes & Noble Books, 1997.

Moore-Ede, Martin, Ph.D. *The Twenty-Four Hour Society.* Reading, MA: Addison Wesley, 1993.

Oliver, Joan Duncan. *Contemplative Living.* New York: Dell Books, 2000.

Ornish, Dean. *Program for Reversing Heart Disease.* New York: Ivy Books, 1996.

Ornstein, Robert and David Sobel. *Healthy Pleasures.* Reading, MA: Perseus Books, 1998.

Pelletier, Kenneth R. *The Best Alternative Medicine: What Works? What Does Not?* New York: Simon & Schuster, 2000.

Ralston, Patricia and Caroline Smart. *Collins Gem Yoga.* New York: HarperCollins, 1999.

Richardson, Donna. *Let's Get Real: Exercise Your Right to a Healthy Body.* New York: Pocket Books, 1998.

Rush, Anne Kent. *Bodywork Basics: A Guide to the Powers and Pleasures of Your Body.* New York: Dell, 2000.

Sharma, Robert. *Monk Who Sold His Ferrari.* San Francisco: HarperCollins, 1998.

Stoll, Andrew, M.D. *The Omega-3 Connection: How You Can Restore Your Body's Natural Balance and Treat Depression.* New York: Simon & Schuster, 2001.

Tomlinson, Cybèle and Vimala McClure. *Simple Yoga.* Berkeley, CA: Conari Press, 2000.

Toms, Michael, ed. *The Power of Meditation and Prayer.* Carlsbad, CA: Hay House, 1997.

Zeer, Darin. *Office Yoga: Simple Stretches for Busy People.* San Francisco: Chronicle Books, 2000.

INDEX

*Encyclopedia of Occupational Safety
and Health, The,* 20
energizing breaths, 110-111
environmental conditions, workplace
conditions leading to stress, 22
ergonomics, 138
eustress, 7
evaluating the source, reducing
information overload, 67
exercises, 123
    choosing the right one for you,
        132
    stretching, 127-128
        flexibility benefits, 128
        practicing, 128-129
    T'ai Chi, 129
        classes, 131-132
        simplicity, 130-131
    yoga, 123
        Ashtanga, 125
        classes, 126-127
        ground rules, 125-126
        Hatha, 125
        Iyengar, 125
        Kundalini, 125
        physiologic responses, 124
exhaustion, 54

F

facials, spas, 138-139
fatigue in the morning (sign of inadequate sleep), 50
Feel Better, 107
fight-or-flight response, 4-5
financial stress, 86
    frugality, 89-90
    long term investing, 90-91
    optimism, 87-88
    paying yourself, 93
    self-assessment, 91-93
    source of household stress, 39
    walking without your wallet,
        88-89

five-minute approach, avoiding procrastination, 60-61
flexibility benefits of stretching, 128
Fritz, Robert (choices), 142
frugality, financial stress, 89-90

G

gender, predispositions to stress, 16
geometric designs (yantras), 115
Glaser, Ronald (researcher, immunologist), 12
Gomes, Paula, Psy.D. (Licensed
Clinical Psychologist), 8
"good" stress, 8-9
    eustress, 7
    versus "bad," 6-7
ground rules
    meditation, 117
    yoga, 125-126
guided imagery, 101-102
    imagining a process, 102
    positive affirmations, 103
    practicing, 102-103
guides, avoiding procrastination, 64

H

Hatha yoga, 125
healthcare impacts of stress, 2-3,
    12-13
    workplace stress, 19-20
healthy diet, maintaining to reduce
    travel stress, 81-82
    airline food, 82-83
    effects of fast food, 82
high-speed world stress, 2
history of spas, 135
holiday season, source of household
    stress, 40
household stress
    awareness of stressors, 44

U-V

unhealthy management styles, 41

visual shorthand, 99
visualization, 95
    contingencies, 99-100
    Mark McGwire, 98-99
    Newton's Law, 100-101
    practicing, 96-100
    preparation for big events,
      97-98
    reducing office stress, 34
    versus meditation, 96-97
    visual shorthand, 99

W

walking through a forest (mindfulness meditation), 119-120
walking with spirit (mindfulness
  meditation), 119
wardrobe, travel stress, 79
weather predictions, travel stress,
  79-80
Web sites
    BarCharts, 72
    Permachart, 72
Welwood, John, Ph.D., 17
win-win solutions, conflict management of household stress, 41-42
workplace stress, 5-6, 19-26
    conditions leading to stress,
      21-22
      career concerns, 22
      design of tasks, 21
      environmental conditions,
       22
      interpersonal relation-
       ships, 22
      management style, 22
      work roles, 22

    dealing with workaholic
      bosses, 26
    healthcare impacts, 19-20
    Internet startup companies,
      23-24
    management, 24-26
    office stress. *See* office stress
    organizational impacts,
      improving productivity, 21-22

X-Z

Yang (T'ai Chi), 130
Yantra meditation, 115-116
Yin forces (T'ai Chi), 130
yoga, 123
    Ashtanga, 125
    classes, 126-127
    ground rules, 125-126
    Hatha, 125
    Iyengar, 125
    Kundalini, 125
    physiologic responses, 124

Jeff Davidson is frequently called to speak at conferences, conventions, and retreats. He has made presentations to 580 groups in North America, Europe, and Asia on topics related to staying productive and competitive, yet remaining balanced and happy while confronting constant change. Comments such as "Best of the Convention," or "Best we've ever heard," represent typical feedback to Jeff's presentations.

Jeff is the author of numerous books, thousands of articles, and nine audio and video programs. Jeff's six-cassette album, *Simplifying Your Work and Your Life* (SkillPath), which he corecorded with Dr. Tony Alessandra, gives career professionals the tools and practical information they need to address the complexity in their everyday lives.

Jeff offers a blend of keynote and seminar presentations on how to maintain balance while remaining profitable and competitive. His presentations include

- Relaxing at High Speed™
- Managing Multiple Priorities
- Overworked or Overwhelmed?™
- Handling Information and Communication Overload

In recent years, several of Jeff's speeches (including "Relaxing at High Speed," "Choosing when It's Confusing," "Overworked or Overwhelmed?," "World Population and Your Life," and "Handling Information Overload") have been published in issues of the prestigious *Vital Speeches of the Day,* alongside those of Dr. Henry Kissinger, Lee Iacocca, William Bennett, Michael Eisner, and Alan Greenspan.

The Washington Post, where he's been featured eight times, called Jeff Davidson a "dynamo of business book writing." Millions of people have read about Jeff in *USA Today,* the *Los Angeles Times,* the *San Francisco Chronicle,* and the *Chicago Tribune,* or have seen him featured on *Good Morning America, CBS Nightwatch,* CNBC, *Ask Washington,* and hundreds of regionally based talk shows.

To obtain a comprehensive list of resources, including additional information on Jeff's keynote and breakout presentations and Jeff's speech availability, visit the Breathing Space Institute's Web site at www.BreathingSpace.com, fax to 919-932-9982, e-mail jeff@BreathingSpace.com, or call Jeff directly at 919-932-1996.